MEDIUM ÆVUM MONOGRAPHS
NEW SERIES

SERIES EDITORS
E. H. COOPER, E. M. KENNEDY,
N. F. PALMER, D. G. PATTISON

MEDIUM ÆVUM MONOGRAPHS
NEW SERIES XXII

CAXTON'S *MORTE DARTHUR*: THE PRINTING PROCESS AND THE AUTHENTICITY OF THE TEXT

by
TAKAKO KATO

The Society for the Study of
Medieval Languages and Literature
Oxford
2002

THE SOCIETY FOR THE STUDY OF
MEDIEVAL LANGUAGES AND LITERATURE

http://mediumaevum.modhist.ox.ac.uk

British Library Cataloguing in Publication Data

A catalogue record for this book
is available from the British Library

ISBN-13: 978-0-907570-15-8 (pb)

First published 2002
This reprint first issued 2015

Typeset by Oxbow Books

TABLE OF CONTENTS

LIST OF ILLUSTRATIONS

LIST OF ILLUSTRATIONS

ACKNOWLEDGEMENTS

The current work grew out of my MA thesis at Keio University, and part of Chapters II and III, in a shorter form, first appeared as an article in *Poetica*, 53 (2000). I would like to thank the editor of *Poetica* for permission to use it in a revised form here. This book is published with the assistance of the Vinaver Trust, to which I owe my sincere appreciation. I am also grateful to The Vatican Library for giving me permission to consult the manuscript of *Nova rhetorica* and supplying me with a microfilm of it, and to the members of the staff of Keio University Library for providing me with necessary information. I would like to thank Mr Shigeaki Iwai of HUMI Project at Keio University for his kind guidance on humanities computing, and the editors of the Medium Ævum Monographs Series and the staff of Oxbow Books for seeing this book through to publication.

I have also greatly benefited from valuable and stimulating suggestions given on various occasions by Dr Lotte Hellinga, Professor N. F. Blake, Mr Brian Donaghey, Professor Yuji Nakao, Professor Tsuyoshi Mukai, Professor Shunichi Noguchi, Dr Valerie Wilkinson, Professor William Snell, and Dr Valerie Edden. Last but not least, I would like to acknowledge my special indebtedness to Professor Toshiyuki Takamiya for his encouraging guidance and supervision at Keio University, as well as to Professor P. J. C. Field who is currently supervising my work at The University of Wales, Bangor, for his support and numerous helpful comments.

INTRODUCTION

Malory's story of the Arthurian world, which he completed in 'THE NINTH YERE OF THE REYGNE OF KYNG EDWARD THE FOURTH',[1] was for nearly five hundred years available only in William Caxton's edition (1485), and was known as *Le Morte Darthur* and thought of as a single romance. Two copies of Caxton's edition have survived: a complete copy in the Pierpont Morgan Library, New York, and a copy lacking eleven leaves in the John Rylands University Library of Manchester.[2] There is no extant copy in Malory's own handwriting. Caxton explains that he printed his book on the basis of a 'copye unto me [Caxton] delyverd, whyche copye syr Thomas Malorye dyd take oute of certeyn bookes of Frensshe and reduced it into Englysshe'.[3]

---

[1] From 4 March 1469 to 3 March 1470. *The Works of Sir Thomas Malory*, ed. by Eugène Vinaver, 3rd edn, rev. by P. J. C. Field, 3 vols (Oxford: Clarendon Press, 1990), p. 1260. Except where otherwise noted, all references to this work are to this edition, cited hereafter as *Works*.

[2] These two copies have almost identical readings. Two sheets have been completely reset, and there are other small discrepancies, which are listed in Vinaver's 'The First Edition', in *Works*, pp. cxxviii–cxxix, and James W. Spisak, Introduction to *Caxton's Malory: A New Edition of Sir Thomas Malory's 'Le Morte Darthur' Based on the Pierpont Morgan Copy of William Caxton's Edition of 1485*, ed. by James W. Spisak and William Matthews, with a Dictionary of Names and Places by Bert Dillon, 2 vols (Berkeley, CA: University of California Press, 1983), pp. 614–16. For the reset sheets, see Vinaver, 'A Note on the Earliest Printed Texts of Malory's *Morte Darthur*', *Bulletin of the John Rylands Library*, 23 (1939), 102–06; Curt F. Bühler, 'Two Caxton Problems', *Library*, 4th ser. 20 (1939–40), 266–71; William Matthews, 'Variant Printing in *Le Morte Darthur*', *Library*, 5th ser. 30 (1975), 45–47; Yohko Nagai, 'Caxton Reconsidered: Variants between the Morgan Copy and the John Rylands Copy of the *Morte Darthur*', *Round Table*, 10 (1995), 1–16.

In this study, the complete copy in the Pierpont Morgan Library, whose facsimile was published with an introduction by Paul Needham, *'Le Morte D'Arthur', Printed by William Caxton 1485* (London: Scolar Press, 1976), will be considered. The phrase 'the Caxton' in this study is short for the copy of Caxton's *Morte Darthur* in the Pierpont Morgan Library.

[3] *Works*, p. cxlv

Thus important editorial questions arise: how different was Caxton's 'copye' from Malory's, and how far did Caxton alter it while preparing it for the press?

In 1934, W. F. Oakeshott discovered in the Fellows' Library at Winchester College a manuscript of Malory's book written by two scribes in the late fifteenth century. While the manuscript is neither Malory's own holograph nor Caxton's setting-copy, it is as reliable as Caxton's text and quite independent of it. This manuscript, now British Library Additional MS 59678, lacks leaves at the beginning, in the middle, and at the end, and differs considerably from the text of Caxton's edition.[4] There are three main differences between the two versions: first, the two texts contain many minor variants, such as different spellings, different word-order and word-divisions, and variant uses of prefixes and conjunctions; secondly, the Roman War episode in Winchester is twice as long as that in the Caxton; and thirdly, while Caxton's text is divided into books and chapters, the Winchester version is divided by *explicit* and *incipit*, and by large coloured capital letters. As Malory says that he finished his book in the ninth year of the reign of King Edward the Fourth, the Winchester manuscript could not have been written earlier than 4 March 1469. Malory died on 14 March 1471, according to a description of the epitaph on a now lost tombstone in Greyfriars, Newgate.[5] The date of the production of the manuscript can be defined more sharply by studies of the watermarks. According to Hilton Kelliher, papers used for the manuscript were produced in France and resemble ones documented by Briquet in 1471, 1477 and 1480.[6] Although only an exact correspondence to the watermark will suffice for precise dating, it is very likely that the manuscript was written after Malory's death,

---

[4] Since its acquisition by the British Library in 1976, the manuscript has been officially called 'The Malory manuscript'. However, there exists a second 'Malory manuscript', a Caxton-derived text written in the second half of the 16th century, listed in *Index of English Literary Manuscripts*, ed. by P. J. Croft, Theodore Hofmann, and John Horden (London: Mansell; New York: Bowker, 1980–), I, pt 2 (1980): *1450–1625*, ed. by Peter Beal, pp. 323–24. In this study, therefore, for the sake of convenience, BL Add. MS 59678 will be referred to by the name by which it first became widely known, as 'the Winchester manuscript', or 'Winchester' for short. *The Winchester Malory: A Facsimile,* intro. by N. R. Ker, EETS SS 4 (London: Oxford University Press, 1976) is used for the present study.

[5] P. J. C. Field, *The Life and Times of Sir Thomas Malory*, Arthurian Studies, 29 (Cambridge: Brewer, 1993), pp. 132–33.

[6] Hilton Kelliher, 'The Early History of the Malory Manuscript', in *Aspects of Malory*, ed. by Toshiyuki Takamiya and Derek Brewer, Arthurian Studies, 1 (Cambridge: Brewer, 1981), pp. 143–58 and 222–25 (pp.144–45 and 157).

and there can be no question of its being copied under the author's supervision, or of any of the minor corrections in the margins being in Malory's own hand.

Oakeshott's discovery, which was reported in the columns of the *Daily Telegraph*, made Eugène Vinaver (1899–1979), who had been preparing a critical edition of Malory since 1931, rush to Winchester.[7] Vinaver had already examined Caxton's two extant copies and Malory's sources, and at the point of this discovery had practically finished his editorial work. Oakeshott recognised that Vinaver was the most competent Malory scholar, and persuaded the Warden and Fellows of the Winchester College to make the manuscript available to Vinaver. Vinaver abandoned his original project without hesitation, and re-started his editorial process using the manuscript as his base text. Thirteen years later, in 1947, Vinaver's first edition, *The Works of Sir Thomas Malory*, appeared. The publication of Vinaver's *Works* gave a considerable shock to the English literary world, in which Caxton's version had been assumed to be authentic. Vinaver proclaimed, as the title of his edition shows, that Malory had written eight separate 'works', and that it was Caxton who irresponsibly edited the 'works' into a single story and deliberately entitled it *Le Morte Darthur* despite the author's original intention.[8]

This innovative, and, as it turned out, highly controversial view was, however, based on an extremely conservative editorial stance. Once Vinaver had decided that the Winchester manuscript was the best basis for an edition, he rigorously followed what it read. Although he admitted that the choice of his base text implied 'no outright recognition of its excellence', he severely restricted emendation, quoting Joseph Bédier: 'L'ayant une fois choisi, nous avons pris le parti d'en respecter autant que possible les leçons'.[9] Vinaver adopted Caxton readings only when they were supported by exceptionally solid evidence. Fortunately, Malory's sources often provided that evidence.

---

[7] W. F. Oakeshott, 'The Finding of the Manuscript', in *Essays on Malory*, ed. by J. A. W. Bennett (Oxford: Clarendon Press, 1963), pp. 1–6 (pp. 4–5).

[8] In his second edition (1967), Vinaver spent two sections refuting Lumiansky and his followers' arguments that Malory's story has a unity, but he slightly corrected his view about the 'unity' of Malory's works, and conceded that while Malory was writing his tales, 'the idea of putting them together and letting them be read one after another did occur to him'; Malory might have started to write with the tale of the Roman War as an independent story, but at some point, he began to consider writing "the hoole book" as Caxton called it. See *Malory's Originality: A Critical Study of 'Le Morte Darthur'*, ed. by R. M. Lumiansky (Baltimore: Hopkins, 1964); Vinaver, Introduction to *Works*, pp. xli–lvi (p. xlv); and D. S. Brewer, 'the hoole book', in *Essays on Malory*, pp. 41–63 (p. 41).

[9] Vinaver, Introduction to *Works*, pp. cxx–cxxi.

Vinaver's achievement was praised by P. J. C. Field, the reviser of Vinaver's *Works*:

> Since the first version of Eugène Vinaver's edition of Malory appeared in 1947, there has been general agreement that it was, as a distinguished reviewer said of the Second Edition, 'one of the outstanding achievements of twentieth-century literary scholarship'.[10]

Scholarly confidence in Vinaver's edition, however, began to be undermined by a number of suggestions that the Caxton version might be more authentic than Winchester. The process started with a paper by William Matthews, which was read shortly after his death by Roy Leslie at the International Arthurian Congress in Exeter in 1975. Then, a fuller version of his study was published in *Arthuriana* in 1997.[11] Matthews argues that portions of the Roman War episode in the Caxton show not only deletions but also additions of new material from the prose *Merlin*, the alliterative *Morte Arthure*, and John Hardyng's *Chronicle*. The passages in question were identified by Field in a later study: he showed that they are particularly numerous in ' "the first page or so" – a page and five lines in W[inchester], a page and two lines in [the] C[axton]'.[12] Matthews deduces that as it was very unlikely that Caxton knew these sources, the most plausible explanation is that Malory himself rewrote the Roman War episode.

This view of Matthews, however, is disproved by the language researches on Malory and Caxton. Yuji Nakao statistically examines the use of language in the Winchester manuscript and Caxton's *Morte*, and concludes that the language evidence is 'clearly in favour of the theory that Caxton revised Book V'.[13] Shunichi Noguchi's research on Caxton's vocabulary also strongly suggests that Caxton revised Book V. Noguchi found in Caxton's Book V words and grammatical constructions that appear elsewhere (in some cases frequently) in Caxton's prose but do not appear anywhere in the Winchester manuscript.[14] Field also reports an interesting alteration in Caxton's Roman

---

[10] P. J. C. Field, 'Preface to the Third Edition', in *Works*, p. v.

[11] Three papers by William Matthews, 'Caxton and Malory: A Re-View', 'The Besieged Printer', and 'A Question of Texts' were first published with an introduction by the editor, Robert L. Kindrick, *Arthuriana*, 7.1 (1997). They are also reprinted in *The Malory Debate: Essays on the Texts of 'Le Morte Darthur'*, ed. by Bonnie Wheeler, Robert L. Kindrick and Michael N. Salda, Arthurian Studies, 47 (Cambridge: Brewer, 2000), pp. 1–107.

[12] P. J. C. Field, 'Caxton's Roman War', *Arthuriana*, 5.2 (1995), 31–73 (p. 48).

[13] Yuji Nakao, 'Does Malory Really Revise his Vocabulary?: Some Negative Evidence', *Poetica*, 25–26 (1987), 93–109 (p. 108).

[14] Shunichi Noguchi, 'Caxton's Malory', *Poetica*, 8 (1977), 72–84; 'Caxton's Malory Again', *Poetica*, 20 (1984), 33–38.

War episode that could have been made only by Caxton. Arthur dreams of a fight between a dragon and a bear, in which the bear is killed. In Caxton's version, the bear is turned into a boar six times. Field says:

> The change must have been deliberate, and it created a bold political allusion: the boar was the badge of King Richard III and the dragon that of Henry Tudor. The allusion would only have made sense in or just before 1485, and it is difficult to see who could have been responsible for it but Caxton himself. His motive seems less likely to have been personal devotion to the exiled pretender than hatred for King Richard, perhaps because one of the first things the king had done after he seized power in 1483 was to have Earl Rivers executed.[15]

It seems then, that both the language of the text and the historical situation support Caxton as the reviser.

John Withrington, who reviews Matthews's theory and examines the two Roman War versions, points out that the passages in the Caxton that were believed to be added from the sources could be found elsewhere than Malory's sources: the Middle English *Brut* and Lydgate's *Fall of Princes*. In Caxton's time, both 'enjoyed immense popularity', and the former is especially significant as it was published twice by Caxton himself under the title of the *Chronicles of England*, in 1480 and 1482.[16] A parallel between passages of Caxton's Roman War episode and the *Chronicles of England* was also examined by Yuji Nakao, who concludes that Caxton 'was able to rewrite Book v on the basis of his exemplar(s) and chiefly the *Chronicles of England*'.[17] Masako Takagi and Toshiyuki Takamiya argue that Caxton consulted the *Chronicles of England* when he divided his Book V into chapters.[18]

Thus, although Matthews failed to prove that Malory was the reviser of the Caxton version, his challenge successfully encouraged Malory scholars to discuss the textual problems of the *Morte Darthur*. Matthews's study has obviously made Malory's textual study a much more contentious place to be.

The next important challenge to Vinaver's *Works* was mounted by the incunabulist Lotte Hellinga in 1977.[19] Hellinga investigated the smudges

---

[15]   Field, 'Caxton's Roman War', p. 37.

[16]   John Withrington, 'Caxton, Malory, and the Roman War in the *Morte Darthur*', *Studies in Philology*, 89 (1992), 350–66 (pp. 359–60).

[17]   Yuji Nakao, 'Musings on the Reviser of Book V in Caxton's Malory', in *The Malory Debate*, pp. 191–216 (p. 209).

[18]   Masako Takagi and Toshiyuki Takamiya, 'Caxton Edits the Roman War Episode: The *Chronicles of England* and Caxton's Book V', in *The Malory Debate*, pp. 169–90.

[19]   Hellinga's discovery was first published in the *British Library Journal*, as the first half

and blots on the leaves of the Winchester manuscript and identified offsets of Caxton's type 2 and 4 on several pages of the manuscript. These traces of Caxton's ink in the manuscript show that it was kept in Caxton's workshop, and so that the actual relationships of the extant texts were likely to be more complicated than Vinaver supposed.

A third challenge came in 1983, when James W. Spisak published his *Caxton's Malory*, which filled a gap in Malory studies as the first critical edition of Caxton's Malory. Spisak's edition is based on Matthews's view that the alterations seen in the Caxton were made by Malory himself, and that the Caxton is therefore more authentic than Winchester. Spisak tried to reproduce what Malory finally intended, on the basis of the Caxton, although he occasionally used the Winchester manuscript for correcting obvious errors. He did not allow for any alterations by Caxton at all. In this, Spisak, though reacting against Vinaver in his choice of the 'best text', seems to have been even more of a victim of best-text theory. As one reviewer says, Spisak's editorial principle was 'too absolute' to solve the problems seen in Vinaver's edition.[20]

In 1990, Vinaver's third edition was published, revised by P. J. C. Field. This third edition is at present the best and the most authentic version of Malory's book. However, practical considerations prevented Field from revising Vinaver's edition as radically as the textual debate suggested above was desirable.

Field pointed out to the present writer that emphasis as strong as Vinaver's on the risks of scholarly endeavour can lead to manifest errors being preserved in scholarly editions.[21] Vinaver was too scrupulous in his editorial policy to use both of the extant texts as fully as they can be used in reconstructing Malory's readings. The purpose of a critical edition, however, is not to avoid risk, but to restore what the author finally intended as far as possible. Although how to define the author's final intention is still a matter of dispute – writings not intended for publication such as private documents, for example, might require different definitions – it is widely agreed that to preserve the

---

of an article in joint authorship with Hilton Kelliher. Her article 'The Malory Manuscript and Caxton', appears in a revised and slightly abbreviated form, with a rewritten conclusion in *Aspects of Malory*, pp. 127–41 and 220–21. All references to this article are from the version in *Aspects of Malory*.

[20] P. J. C. Field, 'Review of *Caxton's Malory*', *Library*, 6th ser. 7 (1985), 366–69 (p. 367).

[21] Field and the present writer discussed the textual problems of Malory in Tokyo on 8 December 1997.

peculiarities of an author's holograph is not the purpose of a critical edition. G. Thomas Tanselle says that 'none of the surviving documents may be a faithful representation of the intended end product'.[22] In the case of Malory, it is not the reading of Malory's supposed holograph, but what Malory intended to write that should be restored.

Revisiting the fundamental Malory texts, the Winchester manuscript and Caxton's printed edition, and investigating what happened in Caxton's workshop, which has not been discussed enough in the context of textual criticism, are the best means of shedding new light on the final aim of Malory studies, the restoration of what Sir Thomas Malory intended to write. This study is offered as a contribution to that end.

---

[22] G. Thomas Tanselle, 'Literary Editing', in *Literary and Historical Editing*, ed. by George L. Vogt and John Bush Jones (Lawrence: University of Kansas Libraries, 1981), pp. 35–56 (p. 54).

CHAPTER I
THE WINCHESTER MANUSCRIPT
IN CAXTON'S WORKSHOP

1. Vinaver's *Works* Revisited

In his Introduction to the *Works of Sir Thomas Malory*, Vinaver first determined the relationships between the texts.[1] That Malory's *Morte* was an adaptation, in a shortened form, of early romances, clearly helped Vinaver in this first editorial procedure. A comparison between Malory's texts and his sources revealed that in some cases Caxton's readings match those of the sources, but not the Winchester readings, and sometimes vice versa. From this, Vinaver eliminated the possibilities of lineal relationships between the texts, as seen in Stemmata 1a and 1b. Instead, he came to the conclusion that the two texts were collateral versions of a common original, as illustrated by Stemma 1c.

Stemma 1: Vinaver's stemmata.

a)	b)	c)	d)	e)	f)
Sources	S	S	S	S	S
(Malory's	(M)	(M)	(M):whycht	(M)	(M)
holograph)			(creature)		
	W	W C		(X)	(X)
Caxton's copy			(X): whyche		
	C			(Y) C	(Y) (Z)
Winchester MS			W: C: that	W	W C
			whyche		

*Malory, X, Y and Z are now lost copies.

---

[1] See 'The Method of Editing' in the Introduction to *The Works of Sir Thomas Malory*, ed. by Eugène Vinaver, 3rd edn, rev. by P. J. C. Field, 3 vols (Oxford: Clarendon Press, 1990), pp. c–cxxvi.

As the next step, this Stemma 1c was developed as Stemma 1d, as a result of evidence deduced from scribal conventions. For instance, Vinaver regarded the following sentence in the Caxton as 'totally unintelligible as it stands':

> And the meane whyle word came vnto sir Launcelot and to sir Trystram that sire Carados the myghty kynge that was <u>made lyke a gyaunt / that</u> fought with sir Gawayn and gaf hym suche strokes that he swouned in his sadel / [2]

These underlined words, Vinaver said, are unintelligible, whereas Winchester reads 'made lyke a gyaunte whyche'.[3] Vinaver suggested that this was originally 'sire Carados that was made lyke a gyaunt whyght', that is, 'Sir Carados, who made like a giant creature'. Then, some early scribe mistook the final 't' for 'e', and made 'whyght' into 'whyche', and this 'whyche', although kept in the Winchester manuscript, was changed to 'that' in the transmission to the Caxton. These variants suggest an intermediate text, an archetype X in Stemma 1d. Another passage, where Winchester reads 'nyght' and Caxton reads 'late', suggests the same conclusion. This can only be explained, Vinaver strongly suggests, by mistakes which occurred in two stages: first, the original was 'sir Lucas saw kynge Angwysschaunce that nyghe (almost) had slayne Maris de la Roche',[4] which is supported by the French source, in which Maris is nearly killed; this 'nyghe' has been mis-transcribed by some scribe to 'nyght', which was replaced in Caxton's workshop into 'late'.

Then, Vinaver further developed his stemma into Stemma 1e. As evidence for the intermediary text between X and W, that is, Y in the stemma, Vinaver quoted the following passage:

> anon [<u>sire Tristram</u> *redde them and wete ye well he was gladde for theryn was many a pyteous complaynte Thenne* <u>*sir Tristram*</u>] said lady Brangwayne ye shalle ryde with me[.][5]

The words enclosed by brackets appear only in the Caxton readings, which Vinaver took as being identical to the readings in X. In the first stage of transmission (from X to Y), an eye-skip occurred between the two identical words 'Tristram', thus Y must have read 'anon sire Tristram said'. Then, in

---

[2] Emphasis added; *Sir Thomas Malory, 'Le Morte D'Arthur', Printed by William Caxton 1485: Facsimile*, intro. by Paul Needham (London: Scolar Press, 1976), sig. s5r.

[3] *The Winchester Malory: A Facsimile*, intro. by N. R. Ker, EETS SS 4 (London: Oxford University Press, 1976), f. 173r.

[4] *Works*, p. 30.

[5] Italics are in the original; underlines and square brackets are added; Vinaver, Introduction to *Works*, p. civ.

the next stage (from Y to W), 'anon sire Tristram said' was contracted to 'anon said', which, according to Vinaver, often happened:

> This type of error, induced by the recurrence of the initial letter, usually occurs between words standing close to each other. It is not likely to have occurred until *sire* and *said* had been brought close together by the omission of the italicized words.[6]

Vinaver concluded that the two mistakes could not have occurred simultaneously, and consequently the first error must be attributed to a text intermediate between X and W, that is, Y.

Finally, Vinaver's stemma developed into Stemma 1f, as a result of evidence inferred from an 'incredible story' in the Caxton:

> and therwith the castel roofe and wallys brake and fylle to the erthe / and balyn felle doune so that he myghte not stere foote nor hand / And so the moost party of the castel that was falle doune thorugh that dolorous stroke laye vpon Pellam and balyn thre dayes [.][7]

Vinaver considered that it was 'incredible' that Pellam and Balyn, who had lain buried under the castle for three days, should have suffered from only minor injuries and that each completely recovered. The Winchester version reads:

> And there with the castell brake rooffe and wallis and felle downe to the erthe And Balyn felle downe and myght nat styrre hande nor foote **and for** the moste p*a*rty of that castell was dede thorow the dolorouse stroke // Ryght so lay kynge Pellam and Balyne iij dayes [.][8]

This suggested to Vinaver that Malory was saying not that Pellam and Balyn were buried under the rubble for three days, but that, because most residents of the castle had been killed, Pellam and Balyn lay wounded for three days. From this, Vinaver deduced that first some scribe in the tradition that produced the Caxton must have inserted 'that' between 'castell' and 'was', and 'it was not until this was done that some grammatically minded reviser, probably Caxton himself, could have tried to restore sense by omitting *Ryght so* and adding *upon* after *lay*'.[9]

Thus Vinaver concluded that X was not the immediate model of the

---

[6] Italics are in the original; Vinaver, Introduction to *Works*, p. civ, n. 3.

[7] The Caxton, sig. d6r.

[8] Emphasis added; Winchester, f. 31r.

[9] Vinaver, Introduction to *Works*, p. cv.

Winchester manuscript nor Caxton's edition; there were intermediary texts both between X and W, and between X and C.

The archetype X in Vinaver's stemma could have brought an editor a stage nearer to Malory. Vinaver, however, made little attempt to reconstruct it, because he was a strict advocate of best-text theory, which was the result of a reaction against a 'full critical' approach to the texts established by Karl Lachmann.[10] Vinaver chose the Winchester manuscript as the best text, in his own words, 'not because it [the Winchester manuscript] is in every respect the nearest to the original, but because it is so in some parts'.[11] As Vinaver was determined to avoid the dangers of Lachmann's wish 'to base his text on a combination of variants', but was offered no alternative technique by his predecessors, he tried to find some 'mechanical' device that would allow him to emend in a more reliable way.[12]

The first kind of emendations approved by Vinaver is corrections of mistakes which are the product of scribal transcription, such as eye-skip. He claimed that scribes make very mechanical mistakes which it is possible to distinguish from the author's own words, and the editor's task is to find and correct them:

> The term "textual criticism" implies a mistrust of texts. It presupposes that in any copied text errors are inevitable and that the critic's main function is to correct them. But no error can be properly corrected, just as no illness can be scientifically treated, without a knowledge of its origin. [. . .] The human agency which is responsible for errors in copied manuscripts is the usually anonymous person known as the scribe, and we naturally assume that a scribe has certain characteristics which distinguish him from any author; [. . .] They [scribes] may have the same sympathies and idiosyncrasies, the same tastes and reactions as the authors themselves. But in one respect they are unquestionably different: the *mechanism* of their work is quite unlike that of original writing.[13]

Vinaver emphasised the mechanical aspect of his theory, that the original composition is a process limited to one plane, whereas the scribes have to

---

[10]   G. Thomas Tanselle, 'Classical, Biblical and Medieval Textual Criticism and Modern Editing', *Studies in Bibliography*, 36 (1983), 21–68 (pp. 57–58).

[11]   Vinaver, Introduction to *Works*, p. cxxi.

[12]   Vinaver, 'Principles of Textual Emendation', in *Medieval Manuscripts and Textual Criticism*, ed. by Christopher Kleinhenz, North Carolina Studies in the Romance Languages and Literature Symposia, 4 (1939; Chapel Hill: North Carolina Studies in the Romance Languages and Literatures, UNC Department of Romance Languages, 1976), pp. 139–66 (pp. 139–40).

[13]   Italics in the original; Vinaver, 'Principles of Textual Emendation', p. 141.

carry their eyes repeatedly from the original to the copy, and from the copy to the original. Thus Vinaver identified six kinds of errors that arose from scribal transcription, which happened from four kinds of eye movement: (a) the reading of the original text; (b) from the text to the copy; (c) the writing of the copy; and (d) from the copy back to the text. These four kinds of eye movement cause the six kinds of errors: misunderstanding of the original (caused by movement a); conscious correction (a); homoeoteleuton (d); duplication (d); contamination (d); arrhythmia (dittography and omission due to break of rhythm in movements b and c).[14]

Vinaver used these categories for emending the Winchester text. Fortunately, the *Morte* is one of those rare texts that can provide an ideal 'third witness' other than scribal errors. Malory was an imitator, sometimes a mere translator, of French and English romances, and therefore his sources can provide clues to many textual problems. Although Vinaver's principles were extremely conservative, this 'third witness' often helped Vinaver avoid the danger of what W. W. Greg called 'the tyranny of the copy-text'.[15] Vinaver, who was already very familiar with Malory's sources, interpreted the passages in which the Caxton differs from Winchester by using the sources, which he asserted were the 'only safe and valid clues'.

Vinaver declared:

> He [an editor] can no longer indulge in a disguised collaboration with the author, borrow his pen, and profess to speak for him. The editor's function becomes that of a referee in the strictly mechanical conflict between the author and the scribe, and his judgment will only be required if there is evidence of the scribe's guilt.[16]

---

[14]   Vinaver, 'Principles of Textual Emendation', p.151. Vinaver is criticised by Henry John Chaytor, in 'The Medieval Reader and Textual Criticism', *Bulletin of the John Rylands Library*, 26 (1941–42), 49–56 (p. 50), for assuming that scribes had 'visual memory' rather than 'auditory memory': a difference that would affect the kinds of errors they made.

[15]   See W. W. Greg, 'The Rationale of Copy-Text', in *Collected Papers by W. W. Greg*, ed. by J. C. Maxwell (Oxford: Clarendon Press, 1966), pp. 374–91 (p. 382) (first publ. in *Studies in Bibliography*, 3 (1950–51), 19–36). Copy-text was always chosen by a genealogical method, that is, by making a two-branched stemma and classifying texts according to 'common errors'. The best-text theory starts from a criticism of copy-text theory, arguing that in most cases, the actual relationships among the manuscripts are inexplicable with a two-branched stemma. The best-text theorists restrict the editor's emendations of a text more narrowly than the copy-text theorists. The different terminology, however, has a common outcome: a text which an editor has selected as the basis of his own edition. In this sense, both texts are in danger of becoming 'tyrannical'.

[16]   Vinaver, 'Principles of Textual Emendation', p. 159.

Thus, in principle, Vinaver demanded a 'critical' edition of Malory made by reproducing one of Malory's texts 'diplomatically', except when the 'mechanical' evidence – scribal errors or Malory's sources – allowed him to emend.

As we have seen, however, Lotte Hellinga mounted an important challenge to Vinaver's edition as a result of her forensic investigation of the Winchester manuscript. Her discovery, although it constitutes evidence about the relationship between the Caxton and Winchester, has been neglected by textual students. The following examination of Hellinga's discovery and Caxton's printing techniques will reveal a more complex relationship between Winchester and the Caxton than Vinaver believed. The relationship will suggest that editors of Malory should resolve to 'speak' for the author using both Winchester and the Caxton equally, not only when there is evidence of 'scribe's guilt', but also when there is evidence of the printer's and his compositors' guilt.

2. Hellinga's Discovery

Lotte Hellinga's discovery suggested that the Winchester manuscript had been in Caxton's workshop.[17] This possibility, however, had already appeared soon after the discovery of the manuscript. Victor Scholderer identified a repair to f. 243 of Winchester that used a piece of an indulgence that Caxton printed in 1489.[18] This indulgence was granted by Pope Innocent VIII in 1489 to contributors to the expenses of a crusade, and printed with Caxton's type 7. There exists another copy of it, in Trinity College, Dublin.[19] As the Caxton fragment lacks the crucial line to show whether it had been used or not, Scholderer who identified it, Oakeshott, and Vinaver all considered that this fragment suggested only that the manuscript had been 'at one time, probably somewhere about 1500, in the hands of a London binder'.[20]

---

[17]   Lotte Hellinga, 'The Malory Manuscript and Caxton' in *Aspects of Malory*, ed. by Toshiyuki Takamiya and Derek Brewer, Arthurian Studies, 1 (Cambridge: Brewer, 1981), pp. 127–41 and 220–21.

[18]   The fragment from the indulgence is now attached to the end cover of the old binding of Winchester. Ker, Introduction to *The Winchester Malory: A Facsimile*, pp. ix–x.

[19]   *STC*, 14077 c. 115.

[20]   W. F. Oakeshott, 'The Matter of Malory', *Times Literary Supplement*, 18 February 1977, p. 193; Vinaver, Introudction to *Works*, p. cii. For Victor Scholderer's opinion, see Hellinga, 'The Malory Manuscript and Caxton', p. 133.

However, Graham Pollard shows that printer's waste, often from indulgences, was used for the reinforcing lining slips for gatherings before sewing, and only specifies unused indulgences.[21] Then, he says:

> Waste paper or vellum can seldom have strayed from the place where it was first considered to be waste; and only at that place it is likely to have been used in a binding.[22]

This suggests there is a reasonable probability that the manuscript was in or near Caxton's premises in 1489 or so.

In 1977, Lotte Hellinga, at the British Library, with the co-operation of the Forensic Science Laboratory of the Metropolitan Police in London, investigated the smudges and blots on the leaves of the Winchester manuscript. Her research with the Level Development Infra-Red Viewer revealed clear differences between the water-based ink which was used for writing with a quill, and the oil-based ink used for printing with metal type. As a result, traces of printing ink became visible in 66 places.[23] Among these, Hellinga in the end identified the offsets of Caxton's type 2 and 4.

The offsets show that the manuscript was in close contact with printed papers which had not dried completely, and which were too heavily inked in the first place. From this, it is possible to picture someone working with the manuscript while the process of printing went on in Caxton's workshop.[24] He would sometimes put wet printed sheets for checking on top of the manuscript. This must have happened between 1480 when type 4 was introduced by Caxton, and the end of 1483, when type 2 went out of use in Caxton's workshop.

Hellinga's discovery coincides interestingly with the earlier discovery of Caxton's indulgence. If the manuscript was in Caxton's workshop between 1480 and 1483, and also some time in or shortly after 1489, there would seem to be a high probability that the manuscript was there continuously during the period when the *Morte Darthur* was in the press. Thus, Vinaver's Stemma 2a on p. 16, which does not allow for any direct connection between Winchester and the Caxton, becomes open to question.

The first question naturally should be, 'how was the Winchester manuscript used in Caxton's workshop?' The fact that Caxton's edition was printed in

---

[21] Graham Pollard, 'The Names of Some English Fifteenth-Century Binders', *Library*, 5th ser. 25 (1970), 193–218 (pp. 195–96).

[22] Pollard, 'The Names of Some English Fifteenth-Century Binders', p. 196.

[23] Hellinga, 'The Malory Manuscript and Caxton', p. 220, n. 7.

[24] Hellinga, 'The Malory Manuscript and Caxton', p. 134.

folio with four sheets created sixteen pages in each quire. The printing process of setting by formes required that pages 1 and 16, 2 and 15, 3 and 14 etc. in a quire should be type-set simultaneously.[25] Therefore, Caxton or a foreman cast off the setting-copy, that is, marked up page divisions in the manuscript in order to prepare for printing. The lack of casting-off marks in the Winchester manuscript clearly shows that it was not used as a setting-copy. Winchester may have belonged not to Caxton, but to an owner who, in Richard Griffith's words, 'would hardly have been happy to have it marked up and taken apart'.[26] It is, as a fifteenth-century vernacular manuscript, rather elaborately made. The major proper nouns which are written in red ink suggest its high value.[27] These considerations suggest that Vinaver, who was not aware that the Winchester manuscript had been located in Caxton's workshop, was right to exclude on different grounds the possibility of Stemma 2b.

Stemma 2: Stemmata suggested by Hellinga's discovery.

a)	b)	c)	d)
S	S	S	S
|	|	|	|
(M)	(M)	(M)	(M)
|	|	|	|
(X)	W	W	W
/ \	|	|	|
(Y) (Z)	C	a copy	a copy
| |		|	|
W C		C	C

The hundreds of passages in the Caxton which have counterparts in Malory's sources but are missing from Winchester exclude the possibility of Caxton's setting-copy having been directly made from Winchester (Stemma 2c). Ingrid Tieken-Boon van Ostade, who believes the idea that Caxton's setting-copy was based on Winchester to be 'almost self-evidently true',[28] tried to find evidence which would support this Stemma 2c in the field of language studies. However, in reality, her findings merely confirmed, in her own words, that 'W[inchester] represents a version of the text which is closer to Malory's

---

[25] Caxton's printing process will be discussed in pp. 32–34 below.

[26] Richard R. Griffith, 'Caxton's Copy-Text for *Le Morte Darthur*: Tracing the Provenance', in *Traditions and Innovations: Essays on British Literature of the Middle Ages and the Renaissance*, ed. by David G. Allen and Robert A. White (Newark: University of Delaware Press, 1990), pp. 75–87 (p. 76). On the other hand, some setting-copies are known to have received discreet treatment by early printers and compositors. See Toshiyuki Takamiya, 'Chapter Divisions and Page Breaks in Caxton's *Morte Darthur*', *Poetica*, 45 (1996), 63–78 (pp. 66–67), and Carol M. Meale, 'Wynkyn de Worde's Setting-Copy for *Ipomydon*', *Studies in Bibliography*, 35 (1982), 156–71 (p. 163).

[27] Ker, Introduction to *The Winchester Malory: A Facsimile*, p. xvii.

[28] P. J. C. Field, 'Review of *The Two Versions of Malory's 'Morte Darthur'*, by Ingrid Tieken-Boon van Ostade', *Review of English Studies*, n.s. 48 (1997), 518–19 (p. 519).

original than [the] C[axton]'.[29] The passages in Malory's sources which agree with only Caxton's text are so numerous and substantial that it would only have been possible for somebody who knew all Malory's sources to insert them.

Is it possible, then, that Caxton was aware of Malory's sources, and used them to create a setting-copy based on Winchester, as seen in Stemma 2d? It is known that Caxton himself was running not a simple printing shop, but a '"full-service" bookstore'.[30] It is on record that Caxton imported some books from the Continent as well as exporting some.[31] Not only printed books but also manuscripts must frequently have been carried out of and carried into Caxton's workshop. Winchester was kept in his workshop for some time, and it is natural to suppose that there were also other manuscripts.

None of the surviving Arthurian manuscripts has so far been identified as directly used by Malory, and how Malory gained access to his various French and English sources from a prison is still an unsolved question. Sir Thomas Malory of Newbold Revel in Warwickshire is the most widely accepted candidate as the author of the *Morte Darthur*, and it has been suggested that this Malory, while he was in prison in Newgate, used the library of Greyfriars, in which institution he was to be buried.[32] However, no one yet has proved that the library in Greyfriars had Arthurian materials; nor has it been explained why Malory was allowed access to the Greyfriars library from the prison.

Richard R. Griffith identified a different set of Arthurian materials which could be Malory's sources. The French royal library collected more than eight hundred volumes during the fourteenth century. In 1425, the library was bought by John, Duke of Bedford, who was acting as regent to the young King of France, Henry VI. In the collection which Bedford acquired, were 'some thirty Arthurian works, including – insofar as they can be identified – every

---

[29]   Ingrid Tieken-Boon van Ostade, *The Two Versions of Malory's 'Morte Darthur': Multiple Negation and the Editing of the Text*, Arthurian Studies, 35 (Cambridge: Brewer, 1995), p. 132.

[30]   Griffith, 'Caxton's Copy-Text for *Le Morte Darthur*', p. 75.

[31]   Nelly J. M. Kerling, 'Caxton and the Trade in Printed Books', *Book Collector*, 4 (1955), 190–99 (p. 197).

[32]   On Malory's time in Newgate, see Edward Hicks, *Sir Thomas Malory: His Turbulent Career* (1928; New York: Octagon Books, 1970), pp. 65–70; on Malory's burial, Hicks, pp. 74–76, and also P. J. C. Field, 'The Last Years of Sir Thomas Malory', *Bulletin of the John Rylands Library*, 64 (1982), 433–56 (p. 440).

French romance used in composing *Le Morte Darthur*.[33] The library could then have descended to Bedford's stepson, Anthony Wydville, 2nd Earl Rivers, who seems likely to have known Malory and who was Caxton's most important patron. A number of scholars have speculated that Rivers was the 'one in specyal' whom Caxton mentions in the preface to his *Morte* as urging him very strongly to publish the book. Thus it is possible that Malory's sources were brought to Caxton's workshop by Earl Rivers.

This can be no more than speculation; but even if all the conditions were fulfilled, for Caxton to have used Malory's sources to correct Winchester would have been a laborious task. The following survey of fifteenth-century book production suggests that it is unlikely that Caxton actually copied the whole text of Malory by hand to make his setting-copy.

3. Two Manuscripts of Malory in Caxton's Workshop

In the fifteenth century, there was a reciprocal movement between manuscripts and printed books; there remain both manuscripts copied from printed books and printed books based on manuscripts. For the manuscripts copied from the prints, errors which are inexplicable without the intervention of the printed book – for example, a mis-transcription of 'people' as 'deople' which can be only explained by a misprint of 'd' as an upside-down 'p' – can tell us that a manuscript was copied from a printed book.[34] Another piece of evidence can be seen in St John's College, Cambridge, MS 178. This is a copy of an edition of Johannes Nider's *Consolatorium timoratae conscientiae* put out in Paris by Pierre Le Dru in 1494. The manuscript has the same collation, the same number of lines to the page, and the identical colophons; it is, therefore, in effect a page-for-page facsimile of the incunable.[35] Manuscripts that were used as setting-copies are easier to identify; the casting-off marks which indicate page divisions for compositors

[33] Richard R. Griffith, 'The Authorship Question Reconsidered: A Case for Thomas Malory of Papworth St Agnes, Cambridgeshire', in *Aspects of Malory*, pp. 159–77 and 225–29 (p. 172).

[34] M. D. Reeve, 'Manuscripts Copied from Printed Books', in *Manuscripts in the Fifty Years after the Invention of Printing*, ed. by J. B. Trapp (London: Warburg Institute, 1983), pp. 12–20 (p. 15).

[35] Curt F. Bühler, *The Fifteenth-Century Book: The Scribes, the Printers, the Decorators* (Philadelphia: University of Pennsylvania Press; London: Oxford University Press, 1960), pp. 34–35.

provide us with clear evidence of their connection. The reasons why these transmissions between different media took place seem to vary case by case. As Reeve suggests, the most plausible reason in every case might be that people just copied a text which was available – 'people transcribed from printed editions when they wanted a text and had nothing else to transcribe from',[36] and vice versa.

It is clear that people in the fifteenth century did not hesitate to copy a text from one form to the other when their material was limited. The statistics, however, suggest more than that. The number of manuscripts copied from printed books seems to be huge. In Bühler's words, 'every manuscript ascribed to the second half of the fifteenth century is potentially (and often without question) a copy of some incunable'.[37] Reeve's example, in fact, backs up Bühler's words. He found sixteen manuscripts of the *Consolatio ad liviam* of which ten certainly and two probably derived from printed editions.[38] On the other hand, printed books set from manuscripts did not amount to very many. While 'there are hundreds, possibly even thousands, of examples [. . .] where we can follow the transmission of a text in print from one printed edition to another', fewer than twenty manuscripts have been clearly identified to be used as printer's setting-copies.[39]

The case of Caxton's second edition of the *Canterbury Tales* is also worth mentioning here. In the prologue to his second edition, printed some six years after the first, Caxton explains that after the first publication, a certain gentleman came to him and pointed out to him that his edition had been printed from an incorrect version. The gentleman offered Caxton a manuscript that was 'very trewe and accordyng unto hys [Chaucer's] owen first book by hym made'.[40] One might expect that Caxton would have printed from the gentleman's manuscript, which he recognised as being superior to his first edition. However, what he did was, by his own admission, to collate and correct a copy of his first edition against the manuscript, and use that as his setting-copy.[41] In other words, Caxton chose a printed book as his setting-copy even when he had another authoritative manuscript.

[36]   Reeve, p. 13.
[37]   Bühler, *Fifteenth-Century Book*, p. 16.
[38]   Reeve, pp. 12–13.
[39]   Lotte Hellinga, 'Manuscripts in the Hands of Printers', in *Manuscripts in the Fifty Years after the Invention of Printing*, pp. 3–11 (p. 4).
[40]   *Caxton's Own Prose*, ed. by N. F. Blake (London: Deutsch, 1973), p. 62.
[41]   Hellinga, 'Manuscripts in the Hands of Printers', pp. 6–7.

Caxton used an autograph manuscript as his setting-copy when he prepared his edition of *Nova rhetorica*.[42] It is therefore clear that Caxton, like other printers, certainly did not mind basing his edition on a manuscript. However, as a setting-copy, he preferred a printed book.

The same has been observed in other early printers. W. W. Greg investigated the first six printed editions of the *Canterbury Tales* (Caxton c. 1478 and c. 1484, Pynson c. 1490, de Worde 1498, Pynson 1526, and Godfray 1532 (Thynne's edition)) by collating the first 116 lines of the 'Knight's Tale' with the manuscripts, and came to the conclusion that it was only Caxton 1478 which was published from a manuscript. All the others, although they were often influenced by other manuscript traditions, were copied mainly from the preceding printed versions.[43] The reason seems to be practical. A printer first had to cast off the text of the setting-copy, that is, count the number of lines and indicate the place where each page started, so that the compositors could work simultaneously on the pages and the press could be always in use.[44] Printed words are obviously easier to count than hand-written ones. Printers, therefore, even those who wanted their editions authoritative, usually preferred to employ the more convenient printed books as their setting-copy.

Since Caxton's *Morte Darthur* was an *editio princeps*, he must have printed it from a manuscript. The nature of that manuscript, however, is the subject of some dispute. If the whole of Caxton's edition of the *Morte* contained as

[42]   See pp. 32–33 below.

[43]   W. W. Greg, 'The Early Printed Editions of the *Canterbury Tales*', *PMLA*, 39 (1924), 737–61 (p. 740). De Worde, for example, seems to have used multiple sources (Caxton's edition and other manuscripts) when he prepared his edition of the *Canterbury Tales*. See William F. Hutmacher, *Wynkyn de Worde and Chaucer's 'Canterbury Tales': A Transcription and Collation of the 1498 Edition with Caxton² from the General Prologue through the Knight's Tale* (Amsterdam: Rodopi, 1978); Thomas J. Garbáty, 'Wynkyn de Worde's "Sir Thopas" and Other Tales', *Studies in Bibliography,* 31 (1978), 57–67; Hellinga, 'Manuscripts in the Hands of Printers'; and Satoko Tokunaga, 'The Sources of Wynkyn de Worde's Version of "The Monk's Tale"', *Library*, 7th ser. 2 (2001), 223–35. Tsuyoshi Mukai suggests that de Worde, when he was printing his Malory based on Caxton's edition, also used Caxton's setting-copy. See Mukai, 'De Worde's 1498 *Morte Darthur* and Caxton's Copy-Text', *Review of English Studies*, n.s. 51 (2000), 24–40. William Thynne's edition also seems to have been based on multiple sources. See Brian Donaghey, 'William Thynne's Collected Edition of Chaucer: Some Bibliographical Considerations', in *Texts and their Contexts: Papers from the Early Book Society*, ed. by John Scattergood and Julia Boffey (Dublin: Four Courts Press, 1997), pp. 150–64.

[44]   See pp. 32–34 below for a full account of casting-off process.

many variations from the Winchester manuscript in proportion to the amount of text involved as in the Roman War episode, we might have to argue that Caxton had rewritten all of his setting-copy. Although Matthews argued that Malory revised the Roman War episode, scholarly discussions after Matthews have proved that Caxton had thoroughly revised the Roman War episode.[45] Indeed, it has been suggested that Caxton added some passages from the *Chronicles of England* that he published in 1480 and 1482 when he rewrote the Roman War episode.[46] However, apart from the treatment of the Roman War episode and the divisions of the story, there are not many striking differences between the two extant versions of Malory's book. And yet, hundreds of passages that have counterparts in the sources but are missing from the Winchester manuscript are preserved in Caxton's book, ranging from a single word to a whole sentence. It would seem very unlikely that an efficient businessman like Caxton would have had a text of a thousand pages copied and collated with several sources, simply in order to insert minor variants like these. It is more natural to conclude that Caxton had two complete manuscripts – Winchester and another copy – in his workshop, and he chose the other copy, which was possibly offered him as a setting-copy, and which he certainly used for that purpose.

The following examination of textual divisions of Caxton's printed books will show that his setting-copy of the *Morte* had some features, which made it very different from the Winchester manuscript or from any hypothetical copy made in Caxton's workshop on the basis of the Winchester manuscript.

---

[45]   See pp. 4–5 above.

[46]   John Withrington, 'Caxton, Malory, and the Roman War in the *Morte Darthur*', *Studies in Philology*, 89 (1992), 350–66 (pp. 359–60); Yuji Nakao, 'Musings on the Reviser of Book V in Caxton's Malory', in *The Malory Debate: Essays on the Texts of 'Le Morte Darthur'*, ed. by Bonnie Wheeler, Robert L. Kindrick and Michael N. Salda, Arthurian Studies, 47 (Cambridge: Brewer, 2000), pp. 191–216; Masako Takagi and Toshiyuki Takamiya, 'Caxton Edits the Roman War Episode: The *Chronicles of England* and Caxton's Book V', in *The Malory Debate*, pp. 169–90.

CHAPTER II
CAXTON'S PRINTING TECHNIQUES: PARAPHS IN FOCUS

1. The Inconsistent Use of Paraphs in the *Morte Darthur*

Two pages from Caxton's *Morte Darthur* reproduced in Figure 1 most strikingly reveal irregularity in Caxton's way of dividing the text; there are pages without any paraphs, and other pages contain as many as ten.

Figure 1: Two pages from Caxton's Morte. *The paraphs are used irregularly.*

maner of truage from Irland for euer/ Whanne syr Marhaus
bad bede hym saye what he wold/ he saide thenne thus agayn
Fair knyght sythen it is soo that thou castest to wynne thob
shyp of me/ I lete the wete/worshyp may thou none lese by me
yf thou mayst stande me thre strokes/ for I lete the wete / for
my noble bede preued and sene/ kyng Arthur made me kny
ght of the table round / Thenne they beganne to feutre theyre
speres/ and they mette soo fyersly to gyders / that they smote
eyther other doune/ bothe hors and all/ But syr Marhaus smo
te syr Trystram a grete wounde in the syde with his spere/ &
thenne they auoyded their horses/ and pulled oute their swer
des/ and threwe their sheldes afore them/ And thenne they las
shed to gyders as men that were wyld and courageous/ And
whan they hadde stryken soo to gyder longe / thenne they lefte
their strokes/ and foyned at their brethes and vysoures/ & whan
they sawe that that myght not preuaile them/ thenne they hurt
led to gyders lyke rammes to bere eyther other doun/ thus they
foughe styll more than half a day/ and eyder were ywounded
passyng sore/ that the blood ranne doune fresshly fro them vp
on the ground/ By thenne syr Trystram waxed more fyersser
than syr Marhaus and better wynded and bygger/ and with a
myghty stroke he smote syr Marhaus vpon the helme such a
buffet that hit went thorou his helme/ and thorou the coyfe of
stele and thorou the brayn pan/ and the swerd stak soo fast in
the helme and in his brayn pan that syr Trystram pulled thry
es at his swerd or euer he myght pulle it out from his hede/ &
there Marhaus felle doun on his knees the edge of Trystrams
swerd lefte in his brayne pan/ And sodenly syr Marhaus rose
grouelynge/ and threwe his swerd and his shelde from hym/
and soo ranne to his shippes and fledde his waye/ and sir tris
tram badde euer his shelde and his swerd/ And whan sir Cris
tram sawe sir Marhaus withdrawe hym/ he said A sir knyght
of the wild table why withdrawest thou the/ thou dost thy selfe
and thy kyn grete shame/ for I am but a yong knyghte/ or
now I was neuer preued/ and rather than I shold withdra
We me from the/ I had rather he dede/ Nay in C yeres/ Syr mar
haus answerd no worde but gede his way sore gronynge/ Well
sir knyght said sir Trystram I promyse the the swerd and the

q5r

Chalenge of Clarance and in his gouernaunce ther came
a knyght that hyghte Elys la noyre/ And ther encountred
with hym kynge Bagdemagus / and he smote Elys that he
made hym to auoyde his sadel/ Soo the Duke Chalenge of
Clarance dyd ther grete dede of armes/ and of soo late as
he came in the thyrdde daye ther was no man dyd soo wel ex
cepte kynge Bagdemagus and syr Palomydes that the pryce
was gyuen that day to kynge Bagdemagus/
Thenne they bede vnto lodgynge and vnarmed hem
and wente to the feest/ Ryght soo came Dynadan and moo
bede/ and Iaped with kynge Bagdemagus that alle knygh
tes laugh at hym/ for he was a fyne Iaper and wel louynge
alle good knyghtes/ Soo anone as they bad
dyned/ ther came a varlet bryng foure speres on his bak/ &
he came to Palomydes/ & sayd thus / her is a knyght by hath
sente yow the chyse of foure speres/ and requyreth yow for yo
ur lady sake to take that one half of these speres / and Iuste
with hym in the felde/ Telle hym said Palomydes I wyll
not fayle hym / Whanne sire Galahalt worshe of this/ he bade
Palomydes make hym redy/ So the Quene Gueneuer the
haute prynce and syre Launcelot they were set vpon scaffoldes
dede to gyue the Iugement of these two knyghtes/
Thenne syre Palomydes and the straunge knyght ranne soo
egerly to gyders that their speres braste to their handes/ Anon
with alle eyther of them toke a grete spere in his hand/ and
alle to sheuered them in ppeces / And thenne eyther toke a
gretter spere/ And thenne the knyghte smote doune spere Pa
lomydes hors and man to the erthe / And as he wold haue
passed ouer hym/ the straunge knyghtes hors stumbled/ and
felle doune vpon Palomydes
 Thenne they
drewe their swerdes and lasshed to gyders wonderly sore a gre
te whyle/ Thenne the haute prynce and syre Launcelot sayde
they sawe neuer two knyghtes fyghte better than they dyd /
But euer the straunge knyght doubled his strokes/ and putte
Palomydes abak/ ther with alle the haute prynce cryed hoo/
and thenne they wente to lodgynge/ And whanne they were
vnarmed/ they knewe hit was the noble knygt syr Lamorak
Whanne syr Launcelot knewe that hit was sir Lamorak he

E1v

Caxton's inconsistent textual divisions, however, have been entirely overlooked in scholarly discussion of his work.

As medieval writings are often preserved only in texts written by scribes who lived long after the original authors, scholars have believed that the textual divisions in these documents could not be authorial, and therefore were not worth serious consideration.[1] It is probably for this reason that Vinaver, who employs modern punctuation, does not explain the system of textual divisions in the Winchester manuscript (nor in Caxton's version).[2] Paragraphing and word division in Spisak's edition are editorial, because 'Caxton's use of paraph marks (¶) does not often correspond to our sense of a paragraph: in many chapters there are none, while in others they interrupt a single line of dialogue'.[3]

The way of dividing a modern prose text varies from sentence punctuation such as the comma, semicolon, colon and period, to the larger divisions such as part, chapter and section, with the paragraph in between.

Sentence punctuation has the oldest history of all, as it has both 'rhetorical' and 'logical' functions.[4] In ancient times, reading was essentially reading aloud; punctuation in the writing was rhetorical rather than logical. Scribes usually did not punctuate the text, and when they did, the punctuation basically indicated how the text should be read aloud. By the end of the sixth century, however, writing became not merely 'the record of the spoken word', but something which could 'also signal directly to the mind through the eye'.[5] By the twelfth century, readers began to feel the need for 'more

---

[1]   G. Thomas Tanselle, 'Classical, Biblical, and Medieval Textual Criticism and Modern Editing', *Studies in Bibliography*, 36 (1983), 21–68 (p. 39).

[2]   Eugène Vinaver, Introduction to *The Works of Sir Thomas Malory*, ed. by Eugène Vinaver, 3rd edn, rev. by P. J. C. Field, 3 vols (Oxford: Clarendon Press, 1990), pp. xix–cxxvi (pp. cxxiv–cxxv).

[3]   James W. Spisak, Introduction to *Caxton's Malory: A New Edition of Sir Thomas Malory's 'Le Morte Darthur' Based on the Pierpont Morgan Copy of William Caxton's Edition of 1485*, ed. by James W. Spisak and William Matthews, with a Dictionary of Names and Places by Bert Dillon, 2 vols (Berkeley, CA: University of California Press, 1983), pp. 601–29 (p. 627).

[4]   Although these functions of the punctuation have been described in various ways, basically categories are twofold: rhythmical and logical; rhetorical and grammatical; elocutionary and structural; or interpretative and structural. See Peter J. Lucas, 'Sense-Units and the Use of Punctuation-Markers in John Capgrave's *Chronicle*', *Archivum Linguisticum*, n.s. 2 (1971), 1–24 (pp. 2–3). Henri-Jean Martin's terminology is employed here, as he discusses punctuation in an historical context. See Martin, *The History and Power of Writing*, trans. by Lydia G. Cochrane (Chicago: University of Chicago Press, 1994), p. 57.

[5]   M. B. Parkes, *Pause and Effect: An Introduction to the History of Punctuation in the West* (Aldershot: Scolar Press, 1992), p. 21.

ostensible help in finding their way about in a highly sophisticated and technical argument', that is, the need for *ordinatio* and *compilatio*.[6] The change in academic reading was directly reflected in the appearance of the page; the presentation of glosses was fully developed in the twelfth century; sub-headings and running titles started to be used: 'the stages in the argument were carefully indicated by means of *litterae notabiliores* and paraph marks'.[7]

The basic concept of dividing a text into parts, chapters and sections – a concept similar to that of our own day – was well established in Caxton's lifetime. When editing the *Morte Darthur*, Caxton did exactly what Vincent de Beauvais had done in the twelfth century: 'for to understonde bryefly the contente of thys volume', Caxton says in his preface, 'I have devyded it into twenty-one bookes, and every book chapytred, as hereafter shal by Goddes grace folowe'.[8]

The antecedents of the paragraph were born together with the concept of *ordinatio* and *compilatio*. Paragraphs in the modern sense originally developed from *notae*, marks which were used to indicate points in a text. Parkes defines *nota* as 'a written character or symbol, not being a letter or numeral, here referring primarily to those used for annotation'.[9] Two *notae* would develop into paragraph marks: the paragraphus (γ Γ Τ Γ Ϛ §), a critical sign used to mark the beginning of a paragraph or section, and the paraph (¶, ¢, //), which derived from the *nota* **K** (*Kaput* or *Capitulum*), a signification for the beginning of a new topic or a point of focus in an argument. Because the letter **K** was replaced by the **C** (*Capitulum*), it became necessary to distinguish this **C** from a capital letter C, and an extra vertical stroke was added to *Capitulum*; **C** became ¢.[10] In this form the *nota* ¢ was developed by the rubricators as the coloured paraph ¶. The double form *virgula suspensiva* // was used as direction for a paraph to the rubricator, but often used as a kind of paraph itself.

Caxton used paraphs in his first book as signs for the beginnings of

---

[6] M. B. Parkes, 'The Influence of the Concepts of *Ordinatio* and *Compilatio* on the Development of the Book', in *Scribes, Scripts and Readers: Studies in the Communication, Presentation and Dissemination of Medieval Texts*, ed. by M. B. Parkes (London: Hambledon, 1991), pp. 35–70 (p. 49).

[7] Parkes, '*Ordinatio* and *Compilatio*', p. 52.

[8] *Works*, p. cxlvi.

[9] Parkes, *Pause and Effect*, p. 305.

[10] On the development of C in the twelfth century see Parkes, *Pause and Effect*, p. 43, and L. C. Hector, *The Handwriting of English Documents*, 2nd edn (London: Arnold, 1966), p. 49.

topics. Although he did not have paraphs in his type 1, which he used for his book the *Recuyell of the Historyes of Troye* (1474), he made rubricators add paraphs by hand, as seen in Figure 2. These paraphs indicate the chapter headings.

In his *Morte Darthur*, too, paraphs are used in this way. When indicating the beginning of new chapters, paraphs are used along with the word 'capitulum', for instance, '¶Capitulum . . .' (see Figure 3).

As paraphs had derived from the letter C, which indicate the beginning of a new capitulum, this use of paraphs by Caxton was solidly conventional. In addition to '¶Capitulum . . .', Caxton begins the new chapters with the words, 'Then' 142 times, 'And' 84 times, 'Now' 77 times, and 'So' 56 times.

Caxton uses paraphs also in order to show some smaller divisions in the text: he uses them in order to divide a chapter into sections (see Figure 4).

Basically, he seems to have followed the conventional rule of scribes; he inserted the paraphs in order to signify the beginning of new topics. The most frequently used words just after the paraphs for the section indicators are the same as those used after the chapter indicators: 'Then' 208 times, 'And' 171 times, 'Now' 56 times, and 'So' 63 times.

Thus some of Caxton's textual divisions can be explained from an historical perspective. He had learned successfully from manuscript culture the concept of textual division such as dividing a text into books and chapters and the use of paraphs to indicate the beginning of a new topic.

However, the use of paraphs as section indicators cannot be explained by scribal conventions alone. As Figure 1 on p. 23 clearly shows, they are sometimes used excessively. For instance, while the chapter divisions are equally distributed throughout Caxton's *Morte*, the use of the paraphs as section indicators appears to be rather inconsistent.[11] Chart 1 and Chart 2 show the number of chapter divisions and the number of paraphs in each quire.

In quire c only two paraphs are used, while in quire q there are forty-three. As we have seen, the most frequently used words for the indication of new topics are 'Then', 'And', 'So' and 'Now'.[12] These words are used at the beginnings of sentences in quire c as frequently as in quire q (see Table 1).[13] That is, in

---

[11] Hereafter, the word 'paraph' will be used only to imply 'paraphs' used as section indicators; paraphs in chapter headings are excluded in the following discussion.

[12] As mentioned above, these words are used after both chapter and section divisions.

[13] Figures are compiled by using *A Concordance to 'The Works of Sir Thomas Malory'*, ed. by Tomomi Kato (Tokyo: University of Tokyo Press, 1974). The Malory concordance was

Figure 2: A paraph added by a rubricator in the Historyes of Troye *(1474).*

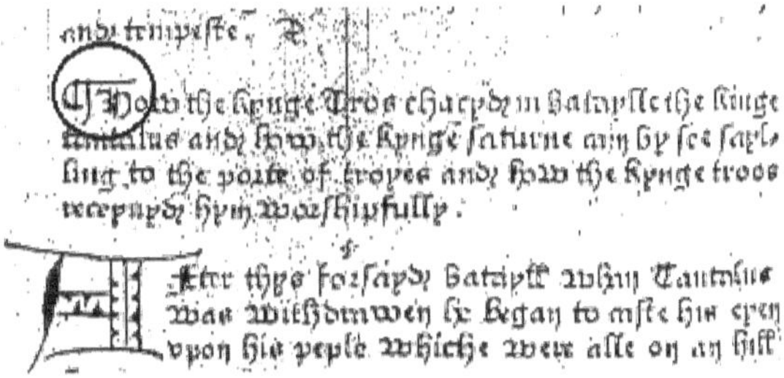

Figure 3: A paraph used as a chapter division indicator in the Morte.

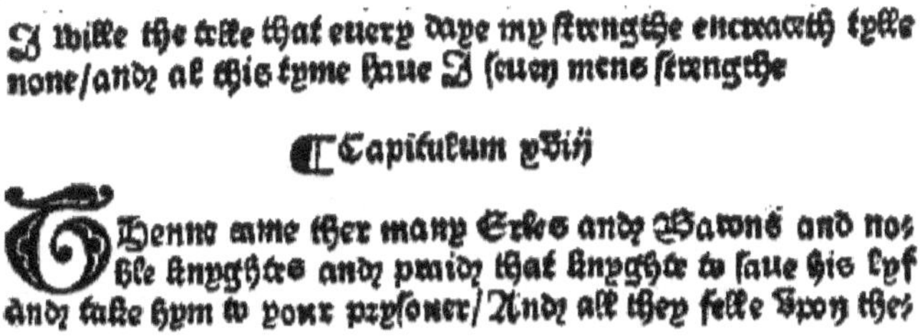

Figure 4: A paraph used as a section indicator in the Morte.

Chart 1: Distribution of chapter divisions in Caxton's Morte.

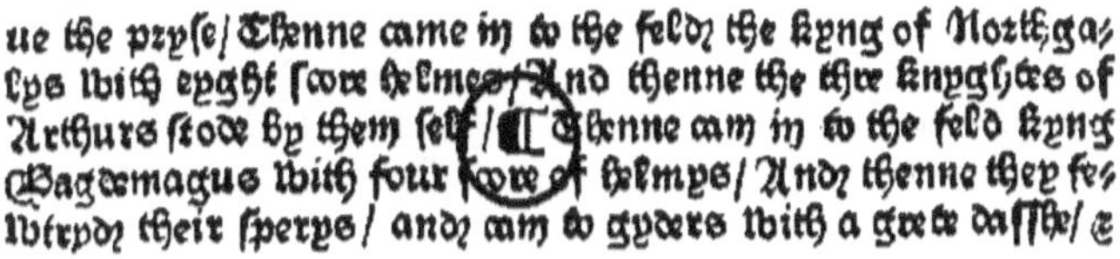

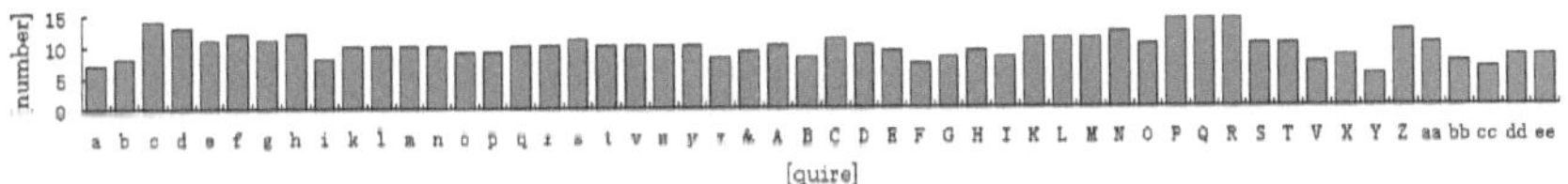

Chart 2: Distribution of paraphs in Caxton's Morte.

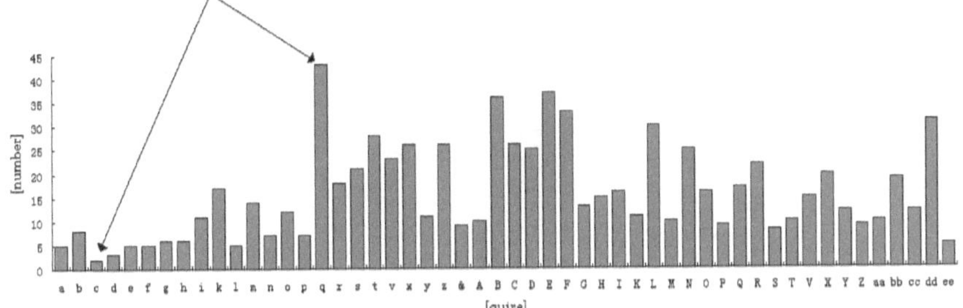

quire c, topics change as often as they do in quire q. This implies that the inconsistent use of paraphs is not the result of the inconsistent divisions of the script itself.

Table 1: Words that begin sentences.

	Then	And	So	Now
quire c	35 times	81	30	9
quire q	35	87	30	4

This inconsistency is also supported by the survey shown in Table 2. The pages of the text have been classified into three types. Those with a chapter division are defined as <type A>, those without a chapter division but with white spaces as <type B> and those with neither chapter division nor white spaces as <type C>. In addition to this classification, each type is further divided into seven categories according to the number of paraphs contained on each page. The numbers after the hyphens indicate the numbers of paraphs. This table clearly shows that the number of paraphs varies a great deal from one page to another. <Type A-1>, <B-1> and <C-1> pages contain only one paraph, while <type B-6+> pages contain six or more. The maximum number of paraphs contained on any page is ten. A collation with Vinaver's edition reveals that many paraphs on <type B-6+> pages are unnecessarily inserted. Fewer than half of the paraphs were regarded as the beginning of a new topic, a paragraph division by Vinaver. In a few cases, the paraph can even be regarded as a 'comma' in the modern sense.[14]

The following examination of Caxton's printing techniques will not only show the reason for Caxton's irregular use of paraphs, but also shed a new light on the textual criticism of Malory's book.

---

compiled using the text of Eugène Vinaver's second edition of *The Works of Sir Thomas Malory* (Oxford: Clarendon Press, 1967) as a basis.

[14] Vinaver, in his *Works*, replaces 33 paraphs by paragraph divisions, 29 paraphs by periods, 17 by divisions between colloquial and narrative style, 6 by comma and 1 by semicolon.

Table 2: Pages in Caxton's Morte Darthur.

<Type A>

Pages with chapter division: 523 pp. (61%).

A-0	A-1	A-2	A-3
278 pp. (33%)	138 (16)	68 (8)	21 (2)

A-4	A-5	A-6
11 (1)	6 (0.5)	1 (0.5)

18 pp.

Table 2: Pages in Caxton's Morte Darthur *(cont'd).*

<Type B>

Pages without chapter division but with white spaces: 120 pp. (15%).

B-0	B-1	B-2	B-3
7 (0.5)	31 (4)	39 (5)	13 (2)

B-4	B-5	B-6+
14 (2)	6 (0.5)	10 (1)
30 pp.		

Table 2: Pages in Caxton's Morte Darthur *(cont'd).*

<Type C>

Pages without chapter division and without white spaces: 197 pp. (24%).

C-0	C-1	C-2	C-3
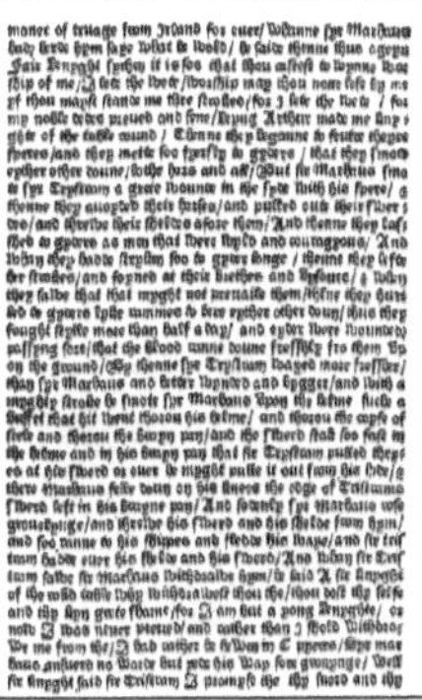			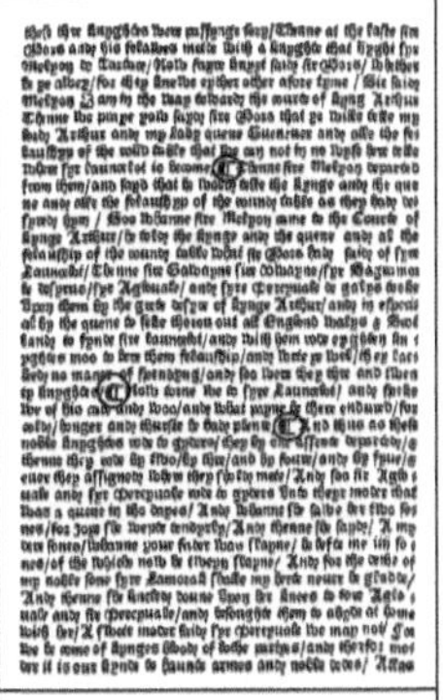
132 (16)	44 (5)	15 (2)	4 (0.5)

	C-5	

	2 (0.5)	
	2 pp.	

2. Casting-off Problems

As we have seen, the printing process of the *Morte Darthur* began with Caxton or a foreman casting off the setting-copy. The book was printed in folio with four sheets creating sixteen pages in each quire, so in order to set sheets by formes, pages 1 and 16, 2 and 15, 3 and 14, 4 and 13 etc. had to be type-set simultaneously (Figure 5). Caxton or a foreman cast off the setting-copy, that is, marked page divisions in the manuscript in order to make this possible. The compositors were obliged to set the text according to the casting-off marks for each page, that is, in exactly 38 lines.[15]

This tradition of setting the text simultaneously, and not in the sequence in which the text was written, came from the conventions of writing. In the early fifteenth century, some manuscript copies were produced by breaking up the exemplar into sections, and giving each section to several scribes.[16] A similar method was often employed in the universities.[17] N. F. Blake also points out that in scriptoria, 'many manuscripts were written on sheets before they were folded and cut to produce the extant pages'.[18]

That Caxton was setting the *Morte* by forme was suggested by the discovery of José Ruysschaert, who studied an autograph manuscript of *Nova rhetorica* by Laurentius Traversanus.[19] Ruysschaert found in the

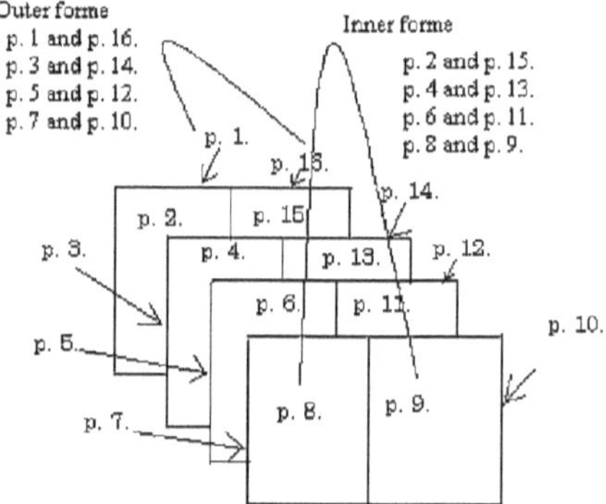

Figure 5: A folio quire of four sheets.

---

[15] As will be discussed, some of the pages in Caxton's *Morte* exceptionally have fewer than 38 lines; there are also pages with 39 lines (see p. 43 below).

[16] A. I. Doyle and M. B. Parkes, 'The Production of Copies of the *Canterbury Tales* and the *Confessio Amantis* in the Early Fifteenth Century', in *Medieval Scribes, Manuscripts and Libraries: Essays Presented to N. R. Ker*, ed. by M. B. Parkes and Andrew G. Watson (London: Scolar Press, 1978), pp. 163–210 (p. 164).

[17] Graham Pollard, 'The *Pecia* System in the Medieval Universities', in *Medieval Scribes, Manuscripts and Libraries: Essays Presented to N. R. Ker*, pp. 145–61 (pp. 153–58).

[18] N. F. Blake, 'Manuscript to Print', in *William Caxton and English Literary Culture*, ed. by N. F. Blake (London: Hambledon, 1991), pp. 275–303 (p. 282).

[19] José Ruysschaert, 'Les Manuscrits autographes de deux oeuvres de Lorenzo Guglielmo Traversagni imprimées chez Caxton', *Bulletin of the John Rylands Library*, 36 (1953–54), 191–97.

Figure 6: Casting-off marks observed in Nova rhetorica.
Vatican, Biblioteca Apostolica Vaticana, latin. 11441, fol. 21v. Reproduced from a microfilm by kind permission of Biblioteca Apostolica Vaticana.

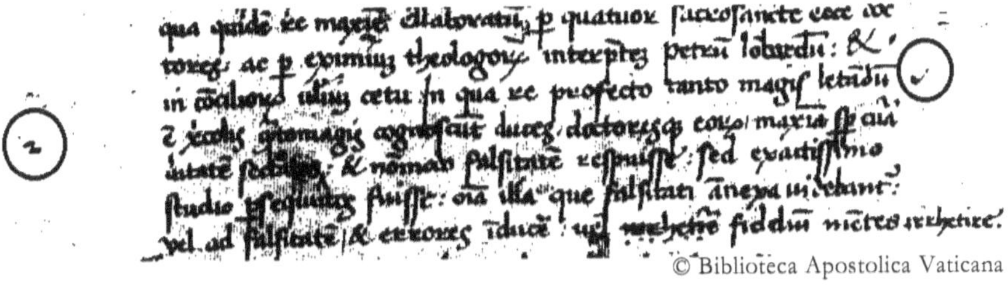

manuscript that certain figures and dashes occurred in a pattern (Figure 6). The number circled on the left hand side meant the beginning of the second page of a quire, and the small mark on the right indicated the end of the previous page. The text was printed by Caxton late in 1478 or early in 1479, and all figures in the manuscript correspond with the beginnings of pages in Caxton's printed edition. From this fact, Ruysschaert concluded that the manuscript had been the setting-copy used by Caxton's compositors. The figures and dashes were the signs of casting off.

In addition, Brian Donaghey points out that in *Boece*, printed by Caxton in 1478, individual types appear more than once in positions which would have been impossible if the pages had been set in numerical order.[20] Setting by forme was economical as it made 'a limited stock of type go further'.[21] Once Caxton had learned this, he naturally would have printed his books by forme.

However, the first step for setting by forme, casting off, was often difficult to manage.[22] The seventeenth-century printer Joseph Moxon (1627–91) dismissed setting by forme as troublesome:

> [N]o wise *Compositer*, except he work on *Printed Copy* that runs *Sheet* for *Sheet*, will be willing to *Compose* more *Sheets* to a *Quire* than he shall have a *Fount* of

---

[20] Brian Donaghey, 'Caxton's Printing of Chaucer's *Boece*', in *Chaucer in Perspective: Middle English Essays in Honour of Norman Blake*, ed. by Geoffrey Lester (Sheffield: Sheffield Academic Press, 1999), pp. 73–99 (pp. 87–88).

[21] Philip Gaskell, *A New Introduction to Bibliography: The Classic Manual of Bibliography* (1972; repr. Winchester: St Paul's Bibliographies; New Castle, DE: Oak Knoll Press, 1995), p. 42.

[22] Gaskell, p. 41.

Letter large enough to set out, unless he will take upon him the trouble of *Counting off* his *Copy*.[23]

However, Moxon still needed to cast off the text in order to determine the total number of sheets that would be needed for one edition. Although he did not have to determine the exact place of page divisions as the earlier printers did, casting off was still a considerable task for him. Thus he described in detail his method of casting off, how to count handwriting. After studying the characteristics of the given hand, a printer would set a typical manuscript line to determine how its length corresponded to the established measure of the line of type. Thereafter, he would count off lines by rotating a pair of compasses.[24]

Casting off was difficult and troublesome even for the skilled printers of the seventeenth century. Calculation gave the earlier printers, needless to say, a harder time, as their methods of printing were still being worked out. A printed copy, or a manuscript of a poem or a verse play, could easily be cast off with accuracy. A hand-written prose text was much more difficult, and mistakes could have happened frequently. Mistakes in casting off were clearly revealed even in the layout of a late and ambitious book like the First Folio of Shakespeare:

> What if it turns out when the time comes to set page 1 that the text meant for this page requires more space than is now left for it? The answer is manifestly that adjustments of some kind will have to be made, that something may have to be left out. Or conversely, if inexact casting off has left more than enough space for the material intended to fill the page, some kind of padding-out may be necessary. That both kinds of miscalculation were common can easily be seen. Some pages are obviously crowded. [. . .] Other pages are unusually "open," [. . .] abounding in unnecessary white lines and wasting space in other ways as well.[25]

A mistake could have serious consequences. Once the text was cast off, the composition and printing went on simultaneously. A compositor had no other choice than solving the problem within the page he was dealing with. When facing the mistakes of casting off, it was necessarily the compositors who were in charge of adjusting the length of the texts.

---

[23]   Italics in the original; Joseph Moxon, *Mechanick Exercises on the Whole Art of Printing*, ed. by Herbert Davis and Harry Carter (1683–84; London: Oxford University Press, 1958), pp. 210–11.

[24]   Moxon, pp. 239–44.

[25]   Charlton Hinman, Introduction to *The First Folio of Shakespeare*, The Norton Facsimile (New York: Norton, 1968), pp. ix–xxvii (pp. xvi–xvii).

3. One Role of the Paraphs

It is clear that Caxton's printing house team had problems in casting off his setting-copy for the *Morte Darthur*. The most interesting problem is revealed by close examination of <type B-6+> pages, the pages with six or more paraphs.[26] Table 3 below compares <type B-6+> pages with the relevant portions of the Winchester manuscript, which, as the only other surviving primary version of Malory's work, is the only possible basis for comparison with Caxton's version. In order to simplify analysis, it is assumed for the sake of the present argument that Caxton's setting-copy was identical with Winchester, and I therefore call words present in Winchester and absent in the Caxton 'omissions' and the converse 'additions'. The omissions and the additions observed in the Caxton, the total length of white spaces, and the number of paraphs included on each <type B-6+> page are as follows:

Table 3: Comparison of <type B-6+> pages with the Winchester manuscript.

[sig. t2r] Omissions: his/ with her/ also/ that/ evir
1.52 Additions: to hym/ there/ Isoud/ soo was he/ that/ in/ for the truage of cornewaile
White spaces: 4.7cm ——————————————————————
¶(8): ¶¶¶¶¶¶¶¶

[sig. D2r] Omissions: Syr/ to/ the/ prynce/ wood
1.75 Additions: hym/ thus/ kynge/ thenne/ a good paas/ neyther/ and syre Sadok that had saued hym
White spaces: 5.9cm ——————————————————————
¶(7): ¶¶¶¶¶¶¶

[sig. z4r] Omissions: and wepte/ sir/ sir/ so/ alyght and/ a/ And/ and/ and/ wolde/ hys/ that
1.98 Additions: And/ of your good wylle/ thenne/ Thenne/ it so happend that/ thenne they/ soo that he/ as though he had ben dede/ thenne/ for whome he
White spaces: 7cm ——————————————————————
¶(6): ¶¶¶¶¶¶

[sig. E4r] Omissions: cam/ tho/ sir/ and/ sir/ sir/ they/ Than/ sir/ And/ sir/ sir/ all/ Sir/ and/ sir/ all/ than/ sir
2.13 Additions: he/ soo/ and they/ so sore/ ellys/ of my handes/ syre/ wylle/ I promyse yow/ and say more worship by yow
White spaces: 11.7cm ——————————————————————

¶(6): ¶¶¶¶¶¶

[sig. E1v] Omissions: sir/ sir/ arson of his/ in sir/ vnto/ sir/ that/ sir/ sir/ And/ sir/ And/ anone/ hym for/ And

---

[26] See Table 2, pp. 29–31 above. All <type B-6+> pages are reproduced in Appendix 1, and the additional words are indicated by rectangles (pp. 77–86).

3.19 Additions: of/ was/ wel/ yow/ of this/ he badde Palomydes/ the/ to gyue the jugement of these two knyghtes/ so egerly/ with alle/ in his hand/ alle to/ to the erthe/ straunge/ a grete whyle/ than they dyd/ hit was the noble knyght/ syr/ that hit was

White spaces: 8.2cm ———

¶(10): ¶¶¶¶¶¶¶¶¶¶

[sig.q3v]Omissions: folowynge/ aftir/ seyde Trystrams/ so/ so/ of

3.24 Additions: syre/ for sorou/ here/ syre/ Thenne yede sir Tristram vnto his eme and sayd/ sir/ sayd he ageyne/ syre/ a messager/ with letters that said

White spaces: 17.6cm ———

———

¶(10): ¶¶¶¶¶¶¶¶¶¶

[sig. q2v]Omissions: sir/ for/ that/ to

3.57 Additions: the/ for oure ryghte/ to/ fast/ the/ and noble/ and renoumed/ of/ dayly/ in euery place/ soo that he sholde/ the/ sende to/ alle/ somme/ that counceylled the kynge not to doo soo

White spaces: 12.4cm ———

¶(7): ¶¶¶¶¶¶¶

[sig. F2r]Omissions: of Cornwayle/ the/ hym/ And/ sir/ all/ thus/ Now/ now/ vs/ yet/ Sir/ sir/ sir/ whyche hyght/ and/ sir/ sir

3.59 Additions: the noble knyghte sire Tristram oute of pryson/ Quene/ the fals traytour/ Thenne/ ful/ the/ wete thow certaynly/ falsly/ this false knyght and traitour/ saunce pyte/ as faste as euer his hors myghte renne/ for sore he was of hym aferd

White spaces: 11.7cm ———

¶(6): ¶¶¶¶¶¶

[sig. B3r]Omissions: is/ Sir/ And/ sir/ but aftyrwarde Now/ seyde sir Dynadan/ sir/ sir/ I may/ for

5.02 Additions: at the laste/ said/ eyther other/ the/ syre/ and noble/ I we/ of fader and moder/ moche/ for the tellyng of your name/ of/ I promyse you by the feyth of my body/ by my will/ be/ therto wille I helpe yow with all my power I promyse you/ doubte ye not/ And certaynly

White spaces: 21.1cm ———

¶(6): ¶¶¶¶¶¶

[sig. R3r]Omissions: that/ sir/ sir

8.29 Additions: goo/ the/ now/ du lake/ the/ saued and/ the whiche I haue told to yow/ for sothe/ alle youre exposycyon and declarynge of my dreme I haue wel vnderstande and herd/ Thenne said the man in this black clothynge/ wete ye wel/ no/ hit/ du lake to/ said the good man/ And/ ladyes/ alle/ and anguysshe/ and only sette his herte in these delytes and deyntees/ & tooke noo thoughte more for his broder syre Lyonel neyther of syre Launcelot du lake his cosyn

White spaces: 14cm ———

¶(6): ¶¶¶¶¶¶

In the first example sig. t2r, from 'his' to 'evir', six words are omitted, whereas the additions are 'to hym/ there/ Isoud/ soo was he/ that/ in/ for the truage of cornewaile', fourteen words. There are 4.7 cm of white spaces in total and eight paraphs. From this point, the total combined length of additions, white spaces, and paraphs will be called the 'surplus part'. The surplus part of this page is about one and half lines longer than the total length of the omissions. The specific difference for each page is listed below the respective signature numbers. In the second example, sig. D2r, the surplus part is 1.75 lines longer than the omissions, in z4r, 1.98 lines, in E4r, 2.13, and the last example R3r has the maximum difference, which is 8.29 lines. The surplus parts are longer than the total length of the omissions on all <type B-6+> pages without exception. On average, the surplus part is about three lines longer than the omitted part.

Note that paraphs are more frequently inserted with white spaces; while eighteen of <type A> pages and thirty of <type B> pages have four or more paraphs, only two <type C> pages have four or more paraphs.[27] In manuscripts, the white spaces around the paraphs are the result of co-operation by scribes and rubricators. A scribe usually wrote a *virgula suspensiva* in a double form (//) in order to indicate to the rubricators that they should insert coloured paraphs.[28] A scribe sometimes left a large space so that a rubricator would easily find the place for his work. For Caxton's compositors, who type-set both the text and paraphs, the white spaces were obviously unnecessary. However, learning from the layout of the manuscripts, they inserted both the paraphs and white spaces, when they wanted to lengthen the text. It follows from this that the surplus parts of <type B-6+> pages indicate that there was likely to have been a mistake in the casting-off process. When originally cast off, these pages fell short of the necessary 38 lines. The compositors therefore lengthened the text, on their own initiative, in order to fill up those pages. Recognising that the cast-off text was too short for one page, they inserted paraphs, created spaces, and added words to lengthen the text to 38 lines.

The text-lengthening in <type B-6+> pages should be reckoned as one of the devices Caxton's compositors employed in order to adjust badly cast-off text. As several compositors were setting up the text simultaneously, it was evidently necessary to finish the pages exactly as they were cast off and create a seamless transition to the following page. If the compositors were faced with a badly cast-off part of the setting-copy, they had to use every

---

[27] See Table 2, pp. 29–31 above.
[28] A history of paraphs was given in p. 25 above.

possible technique in order to match text to the page. It is important to note when discussing <type B-6+> pages that in most cases the fundamental meaning has not been changed by these additional words. The additional words act as paraphrases, repetitions or modifiers.

Fifteenth-century compositors in general frequently altered the readings of their setting-copy. Carol Meale's research on the setting-copy of de Worde suggests that 'the compositor was [. . .] left to effect further changes as he went along'.[29] Lotte Hellinga's study of the manuscript of a Dutch translation of Raoul le Fèvre's *History of Jason* also suggests that the compositors of this period had great freedom in the production of texts. Since the casting-off marks on this manuscript of *Jason* agree with the edition printed in Haarlem in 1485 by Jacob Bellaert, there is clearly a direct link between the manuscript and the printed text. However, Hellinga points out that there are many textual variants between the two texts.[30] If it had not been for the casting-off marks, these two texts would have been assumed to have had a collateral relationship.

This also seems to hold true for Caxton's compositors. Most of the additional words in <type B-6+> pages can be interpreted as being examples of padding which were made by Caxton's compositors.[31] In <type B-6+> pages, for example, there are as many as seven examples of doublets, repetitions and pairs of double words which do not appear in Winchester. Doublets were not something new to Caxton. Without doubt, Malory, Caxton and many fifteenth-century English writers often used doublets. Shunichi Noguchi reveals that without taking into account the Roman War episode, 'there are just as many paired words in Caxton's variants as those which in the relevant passages solely belong to the Winchester MS – Caxton's fifty-six as against Winchester's fifty-seven'.[32] However, when we turn to Caxton's own prose, Caxton's

[29] Carol M. Meale, 'Wynkyn de Worde's Setting-Copy for *Ipomydon*', *Studies in Bibliography*, 35 (1982), 156–71 (p. 168).

[30] Lotte Hellinga, 'The Malory Manuscript and Caxton', in *Aspects of Malory*, ed. by Toshiyuki Takamiya and Derek Brewer, Arthurian Studies, 1 (Cambridge: Brewer, 1981), pp. 127–41 and 220–21 (p. 136).

[31] Jeremy J. Smith's linguistic studies on Caxton's translations and on the *Morte* interestingly reveal that 'there is no need to suppose other linguistic layers belonging to his [Caxton's] compositors'. Caxton's compositors might have used similar dialect to that of Caxton's, or, since some foreigners such as Wynkyn de Worde worked for Caxton, it is possible that his compositors were easily affected by their master's language. Therefore, it is reasonable to identify 'Caxtonian' language with the language of his compositors. See Jeremy J. Smith, 'Some Spellings in Caxton's Malory', *Poetica*, 24 (1986), 58–63 (p. 62).

[32] Shunichi Noguchi, 'Caxton's Malory Again', *Poetica*, 20 (1984), 33–38 (pp. 33–34).

preference for doublets seems to be stronger than that of Malory's. Noguchi lists examples of doublets found in Caxton's earlier writings and concludes that 'Caxton is least expected to abandon and give up, "his excessive use of pairs of synonymous words"'.[33] Caxton's preference for doublets becomes particularly obvious, given the fact that he re-wrote the Roman War episode in the *Morte Darthur*. Caxton's Roman War episode abounds in doublets:

> It is almost as though Caxton says nothing once that can be said twice. Done excessively, this use of doublets is distinctly un-Malorian [. . .]. Frequent doublets are not at all a feature of Malory's straightforward prose.[34]

According to McCarthy, there are more than 100 examples of doublets in the Roman War episode in Caxton's version.

Two examples of doublets in <type B-6+> pages are found in sig. q2v:[35]

    sig. q2v, 376/32–36
        19   ¶Thenne made kynge marke grete sorou whan he vnderstood
        20   that the good ***and noble*** knyghte sire Marhaus was come /
        21   For they knewe no knyght that durste haue adoo with hym /
        22   For at that tyme syre Marhaus was called one of the famo-
        23   sost ***and renoumed*** knyghtes of the world------------------------

The expression 'good and noble' appears only four times (with variations) out of 440 'noble' and 949 'good' found in the Winchester manuscript.[36] It is, however, interesting that in Caxton's <type B-6+> pages, 'and noble' are inserted twice after 'good'. The other example is seen in sig. B3r, line 31, 596/33.

---

[33] Shunichi Noguchi, 'Caxton's Malory', *Poetica*, 8 (1977), 72–84 (p. 75).

[34] Terence McCarthy, 'Caxton and the Text of Malory's Book 2', *Modern Philology*, 71 (1973), 144–52 (p. 149).

[35] All citations from the *Morte* in this section are taken from *Sir Thomas Malory, 'Le Morte D'Arthur', Printed by William Caxton 1485: Facsimile*, intro. by Paul Needham (London: Scolar Press, 1976); the variants found only in the Caxton are indicated by italicised bold letters. The white spaces in the Caxton are presented by '------'. Caxton's signature numbers are followed by page and line numbers of Vinaver's *Works*. Vinaver's interpretations are shown using his own marks. Vinaver put all the Caxton readings in his critical apparatus 'exclusive of differences of spelling and minor differences of wording'. He marked the Caxton readings with asterisks * when the Caxton readings are either clearly preferable to those of the base text, or likely to throw some light upon those. See Vinaver, Introduction to *Works*, pp. cxxii–cxxiii. All the <type B-6+> pages are reproduced in Appendix 1 (pp. 77–86) with line numbers; the additions are marked with rectangle.

[36] Four examples are as follows: 'good and noble' 688/15 and 793/12; 'the good noble knyghtes' 467/6; and 'a good knyght and a noble' 694/7.

The doublet, 'famosost and renoumed', on the other hand, does not appear at all in Winchester. It should be emphasised here that, according to Mizobata's concordance, out of twenty-two instances of 'renome' found in Caxton's own prologues and epilogues, fifteen are used as doublets, four of them with 'fame'.[37] On the other hand, in Winchester, the word 'famosost' is only used twice.[38] This doublet, thus, seems to be a Caxtonian rather than a Malorian characteristic. Caxton or the compositor, finding the unusual word 'famosost' in Malory's text, would have added 'and renoumed' and made the word into a familiar doublet expression.

The expression 'false traitor' is added twice in sig. F2r, line 9 and line 35:

> sig. F2r, 683/35–684/1, 684/25–30
>
> 9   alle this whyle kynge Marke ***the fals traytour*** is in pryson /
>
> 31   Thenne sir Bleoberis cryed a lowde and said thus / make ***the***
> 32   redy thou fals traytour knyghte Breuse saunce pyte / for ***wete***
> 33   ***thow certaynly*** I wille haue adoo with the to the vtteraunce
> 34   for the noble knyghtes and ladyes that thou hast ***falsly*** bi-
> 35   trad---------------¶Whanne this ****false knyght and traitour***
> 36   Breuse ****saunce pyte*** herde hym saye soo /

This expression 'false traitor' is so common that it can easily be inserted by any compositor. In particular, the latter example (l. 35) is very likely to have been added by a compositor because exactly the same words are found in the line above: 'thou fals traytour knyghte Breuse saunce pyte' (l. 32). The 'falsly' in l. 34 can be recognised as an example of repetition. Although Vinaver considers that the Caxton readings are preferable at these places, and places asterisks by the phrases 'false knyght and traitour' (l. 35), and 'saunce pyte' (l. 36), all these synonyms should be interpreted as one of the devices used to lengthen the text. While none of the words derived from 'certain' appears in Winchester, in Caxton's own prose, 'certaynly' and its derivatives are used 25 times.[39] This word 'certaynly' is clearly Caxtonian. Furthermore, the same word 'certaynly' is inserted in another <type B-6+> page, sig. B3r. These words, thus, can be interpreted as a result of the compositor's space-filling.[40]

---

[37] There are variants such as 'renomed', 'renomme', 'renommed' and 'renomee'. See *A Concordance to Caxton's Own Prose,* ed. by Kiyokazu Mizobata (Tokyo: Shohakusha, 1990); Caxton's concordance is based on N. F. Blake's *Caxton's Own Prose* (London: Deutsch, 1973).

[38] The other occasion is 'moste famous knyght' in 1232/9.

[39] The variants are 'certayn', 'certayne', 'certaynely', 'certaynly' and 'certeyn'.

[40] There is another example of doublet '***saued and*** rescowed' in sig. R3r.

The fact that other Caxtonian doublets are found in relatively less crowded pages – the pages which might have required lengthening of the text – also supports the theory that the doublets seen in <type B-6+> pages were inserted by Caxton's compositors. Noguchi identifies twenty Caxtonian doublets elsewhere in <type B-6+> pages.[41] Out of twenty doublets, only two of them are found in pages without any paraphs or white spaces, <type C-0> pages. The others are found either in pages with chapter divisions or with white spaces. In both cases, the cast-off text in the setting-copy was far too short for Caxton's 38-line page.[42]

We must therefore assume that Caxton's compositors were responsible even for adding totally new words when they needed to lengthen the text and to 'make it look like a page filled to normal length, a "seamless" transition to the following page'.[43] Taken together, the fact that the surplus parts on every page are longer than the omitted parts, and that the meaning of the text has not been changed by the added words, seem to indicate that the only role of the surplus parts in <type B-6+> has been to lengthen the text.[44]

4. Caxton's Copy-Fitting Devices

Lotte Hellinga's study also supports the conclusion of the previous section that the role of the surplus parts in <type B-6+> was to lengthen the text. She points out that the variants of Caxton's *Morte Darthur* from the Winchester manuscript are disproportionately seen at a page division.[45] The compositors seem sometimes to have found towards the end of a page that the cast-off text of the setting-copy was either too short or too long to fit in Caxton's 38 lines, and at this point they either added or deleted some words. This

---

[41] Noguchi lists some examples in his 'Caxton's Malory' and 'Caxton's Malory Again'. In addition, he introduces some more examples of Caxtonian doublets in 'The Winchester Malory as a Scribal (Rather Than an Edited) Text', a paper presented in the Symposium, 'Textual Problems of Malory's *Morte Darthur*', at the Thirteenth Congress of the Japan Society for Medieval English Studies held in Tokyo, 7 December 1997. In this present discussion, the examples found in Book 5 are excluded.

[42] <Type A-0>, 5 pages; <A-1>, 4; <A-2>, 3; <A-3>, 1; <A-4>, 1; <B-2>, 2; and <B-3>, 2.

[43] Lotte Hellinga, *Caxton in Focus: The Beginning of Printing in England* (London: British Library, 1982), p. 94.

[44] Some other examples of additions observed in <type B-6+> pages are discussed in Appendix 2 (pp. 87–92).

[45] Hellinga, *Caxton in Focus*, p. 92.

Chart 3: Spatial distribution of paraphs, white spaces and additions
in <type B-6+> pages.

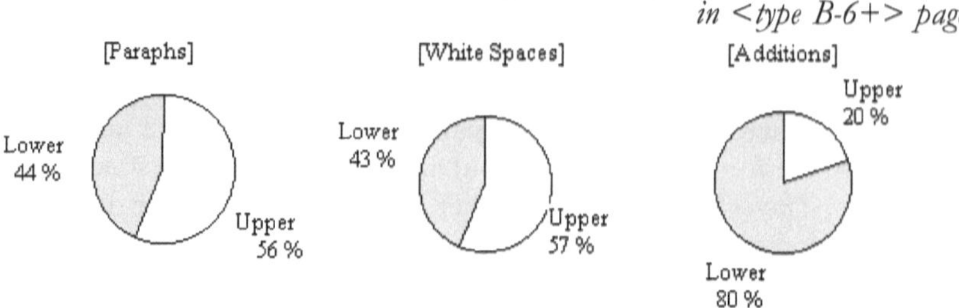

tendency is also observed in <type B-6+> pages. In Chart 3, the 38 lines of each page were divided into half, 19 lines each, and the distribution of paraphs, white spaces and additions in each section are examined. These diagrams show that, while paraphs and white spaces are equally distributed from the beginning to the end of a page, word additions are seen mainly in the later half of pages. It seems therefore that the compositors first used the paraphs and white spaces to lengthen the text, and then at the end of the page, as the second device, added some words, if their copy still did not fit the page.

Toshiyuki Takamiya has also shown that a good deal of the text in the setting-copy was changed by the hands of compositors at the end of pages so that a page would end at the exact point indicated in the setting-copy. Takamiya focuses on the repetition seen at the page break from sig. T3r to T3v:

> The Caxton, sig. T3r: Thenne felte he many handes <u>aboute hym</u> whiche tooke hym vp / and bare hym oute *of the chamber dore* / <u>withoute ony amendynge of his swoune</u> / *and lefte hym there semyng dede to*
>
> The Caxton, sig. T3v: *of the chamber dore and lefte hym there semynge dede to* al peple / Soo vpon the morowe
>
> Winchester, f. 401v: Than felte he many hondys whych toke hym vp and bare hym oute of the chambir doore and leffte hym þer semynge dede to all people So vppon the morow.[46]

The end of T3r contains not only a repetition of the words seen at the beginning of T3v (italics), but also words which are not seen in the Winchester

---

[46] Emphasis added; transcribed from the facsimile of the Caxton, and *The Winchester Malory: A Facsimile*, intro. by N. R. Ker, EETS SS 4 (London: Oxford University Press, 1976).

manuscript (underlined): 'aboute hym' and 'withoute ony amendynge of his swoune'. Takamiya reconstructs the reading of the setting-copy by deleting the words which were repeated as a result of casting-off problems. Takamiya, using the Malory and the Caxton concordances, points out that while the gerund 'amendynge' is not used anywhere else in the Winchester manuscript, the word 'amende' is used in Caxton's own prose, 'as many as sixteen times, with "amendement" and "amendyng" appearing once each'.[47] The reading of the setting-copy which was established using the evidence of Caxton's copy-fitting problems is, therefore, supported by the characteristics of 'Caxtonian' and 'Malorian' languages.

The irregular layout of pages other than <type B-6+> pages also suggests that compositors were attempting to deal with the badly cast-off text. Although there are usually 38 lines in each page, many pages have an irregular number of lines. First, when book or chapter divisions are placed at the page divisions, some of the pages before these divisions are several lines short; there is even a page with only 22 lines. Furthermore, 7 pages have 39 lines;[48] 14 of <type B> pages, 17 <type A> pages and 3 <type C> pages have only 37 lines. These would be the result of compositors' silent deception; they presumably hoped that a difference of only one line would escape notice, and neglected their duty to lengthen or shorten the cast-off text to exactly 38 lines.

In Table 4, all <type A> pages, i.e., pages with chapter divisions, are arranged into six categories according to the number of blank lines used around the chapter division indicators.[49] This table shows that while at times chapter divisions used no lines at all, at other times they used as many as five lines, the average being three lines, that is, two blank lines and one line for the chapter number.

Takamiya discusses the chapter divisions that used no lines, intralinear chapter divisions, in Caxton's *Morte Darthur*.[50] Although the woodcut letter on the left hand side and the chapter number on the right tell us that the intralinear chapter division exemplified in Table 4 includes a chapter division,

<hr>

[47] Toshiyuki Takamiya, 'Editor / Compositor at Work: The Case of Caxton's Malory', in *Arthurian and Other Studies Presented to Shunichi Noguchi*, ed. by Takashi Suzuki and Tsuyoshi Mukai (Cambridge: Brewer, 1993), pp. 143–51 (p. 150).

[48] The following pages have 39 lines: sig. l1r, m4v, m5r, x8r, K5v, U2v and ee5v.

[49] Chapter divisions that accord with page breaks are not considered in this table.

[50] Toshiyuki Takamiya, 'Chapter Divisions and Page Breaks in Caxton's *Morte Darthur*', *Poetica*, 45 (1996), 63–78 (pp. 68–69).

Table 4: Layout of Caxton's chapter divisions.

Intralinear chapter divisions: 28 pp (7 %)	2 blank lines: 176 (44)
Chapter divisions without a blank line: 49 (12)	3 blank lines: 103 (25)
1 blank line: 35 (9)	4 blank lines: 13 (3)

there are no lines inserted to indicate where it is. According to Takamiya, this kind of intralinear chapter division seems to have been the result of compositors' efforts to adjust to the page a cast-off text that they had found to be far too long.

These problems seem to have arisen in Caxton's workshop with other texts as well. Brian Donaghey points out that the *Boece* printed by Caxton in 1478 also reveals problems of estimation. Since the *Boece* consists of labelled sections of text, Caxton uses the chapter headings as in the *Morte*, but follows the manuscript practice of quoting the start of the Latin text as an identifier of each chapter. The compositors lengthened or shortened these quotations to fit the pages as necessary; some of these quotations are therefore disproportionately long and intensive compared to the amount of English text which follows them.[51]

---

[51] Donaghey, 'Caxton's Printing of Chaucer's *Boece*', pp. 88–91.

That Caxton's compositors of the *Morte*, who type-set <type B-6+> pages, had a very badly cast-off text as their setting-copy is also supported by the survey of <type C-0> pages, which provide a striking contrast to <type B-6+> pages. Table 5 sets out the results of an examination of 37 <type C-0> pages. These were compared with the Winchester manuscript, and the numbers of words 'omitted and added' were examined; on average, in <type C-0> pages, 17 words have been omitted and 18 words have been added. The number of additional words, that is, is nearly the same as that of omitted words. On the other hand, in <type B-6+> pages, while only 10 words on average have been omitted, 35 words, 3.5 times that number, have been added. This considerable difference clearly shows the necessity of text lengthening in <type B-6+> pages.

The type of 'and' used supports the same conclusion; three kinds of 'and' – that is, ampersand, 'and' without flourish and 'and' with flourish – are used in the *Morte* (Table 6). An obvious intention of using the 'and' to lengthen the text can be detected in their use in <type B-6+> pages. Three of these pages (t2r, D2r and q3v) do not contain any ampersands; three of them (q2v, F2r and B3r) contain only one; and four (z4r, E4r, E1v and R3r) have two. Moreover, on all pages but sig. t2r and q2v, the

Table 5: Omissions and additions in <C-0> and <B-6+> pages.

	Omissions	Additions
<type C-0>	17 words	18 words
<type B-6+>	10 words	35 words

Table 6: Three kinds of 'and' in <B-6+> pages.

	ampersand	unflourished	flourished
t2r	0	23	8
D2r	0	2	23
q3v	0	1	14
q2v	1	9	7
F2r	1	2	18
B3r	1	2	19
z4r	2	9	17
E4r	2	0	23
E1v	2	2	24
R3r	2	1	21

flourished 'and' is used more frequently than unflourished 'and'.

Table 7:
Paraphs in the Caxton, and // in Winchester.

	Correspond	Do not Correspond
<type C-1>	20 (47 %)	23 (53 %)
<type B-6+>	22 (30 %)	50 (70 %)

On the other hand, there are 12 pages which contain 20 or more ampersands per page in Caxton's *Morte*, and 6 of them are <type A-0> pages; 1 is a <type B-0> page; and 5 are <type C-0> pages. That is, none of these pages contain any paraphs. While ampersands are scarcely used in the pages with many paraphs, the paraphs are scarcely used in the pages with many ampersands. Choosing between the abbreviation mark ampersand, unflourished 'and' and flourished 'and' seems to have been the easiest device for shortening and lengthening the amount of the text.[52]

In addition, the comparison of paraphs in Caxton's book with the use of *virgula suspensiva* in the double form (//) in the Winchester manuscript suggests that the paraphs in <type B-6+> pages were not taken from the setting-copy, but originally inserted by Caxton's compositors. As was argued above, the double *virgula suspensiva* was first used by scribes as a direction to the rubricators for a paraph, but later was often used to 'fulfil the function of the paraph itself'.[53] In <type C-1> pages, which form a contrast in their appearance to <type B-6+> pages, there are as many paraphs which correspond to *virgulae* in Winchester as those which do not.[54] On the other hand, in <type B-6+> pages, 70 % of the paraphs do not correspond to the *virgulae* (Table 7). This evidence provides independent confirmation for the conclusion that Vinaver drew from the substantives of the two texts: it suggests that the Winchester manuscript and Caxton's book derive independently from a common original. It also suggests that Caxton's setting-copy may have had similar, if not identical punctuation to that seen in the Winchester manuscript. That the paraphs in <type B-6+> pages correspond less frequently to the *virgulae* in Winchester than the paraphs in the <C-1> pages supports the probability that the paraphs in <B-6+> pages were

---

[52]   Hitoshi Isaka and Yoshihiro Shiratori also discuss the use of 'and' in Caxton's *Morte Darthur*. See 'A Study of "and" in Caxton's *Morte Darthur*', *Round Table*, 11 (1996), 14–30 [in Japanese].

[53]   Parkes, *Pause and Effect*, p. 305. See also p. 25 above.

[54]   Sig. h8v is out of consideration here, as it corresponds to Caxton's Roman War episode.

originally introduced to the text in Caxton's workshop. The skilled compositors who set up the <type B-6+> pages were able to judge that the cast-off text was far too short for one page. Aware that paraphs should be placed where they would act as punctuation, Caxton's compositors used paraphs, white spaces, and additional words to lengthen the short cast-off text of the setting-copy to the required 38 lines.

We may ask why Caxton or his foreman made such a large mis-estimation when casting off the setting-copy. A detailed study of Caxton's chapter divisions in the following chapter will reveal not only the reasons for the mis-estimation during the casting-off process, but also some additional irregular aspects of Caxton's setting-copy.

CHAPTER III
CAXTON'S IRREGULAR SETTING-COPY

1. Caxton's Inconspicuous Editorial Hand

In his preface to the *Morte Darthur*, Caxton says that he divided the text into books and chapters:

> And for to understonde bryefly the contente of thys volume I [Caxton] have devyded it into twenty-one bookes, and every book chapytred [. . .][1]

As most of the coloured initial letters in Winchester coincide with Caxton's book and chapter divisions, there is a possibility that some book or chapter divisions in the Caxton were prompted by features in the archetype. However, Caxton introduced about five times as many divisions as those found in Winchester. Caxton's setting-copy clearly did not have as many divisions as the Caxton, and it was Caxton himself, as he claimed, who divided the text. Caxton or a foreman, therefore, looked over the setting-copy of the *Morte Darthur* at least twice before it was sent round to the compositors: first he read the text and marked chapter divisions, and secondly he cast off the text, i.e., estimated the amount of the text required for each page and marked the page breaks. Because the setting-copy contained no book or chapter divisions, Caxton or a foreman would, during the casting-off process, cast off pages determined as needing chapter divisions with only 35 lines of text. This allowed three blank lines for the chapter division as illustrated in Figure 7.

As was pointed out in the previous chapter, while chapter divisions with two blank lines and a line for a chapter number indicator are the most common type in the Caxton, there are also intralinear chapter divisions, as a result of compositors' efforts to adjust excessive cast-off text.[2] In the

---

[1] *The Works of Sir Thomas Malory*, ed. by Eugène Vinaver, 3rd edn, rev. by P. J. C. Field, 3 vols (Oxford: Clarendon Press, 1990), p. cxlvi.

[2] See pp. 43–44 above.

Figure 7: A typical chapter division and an intralinear chapter division.

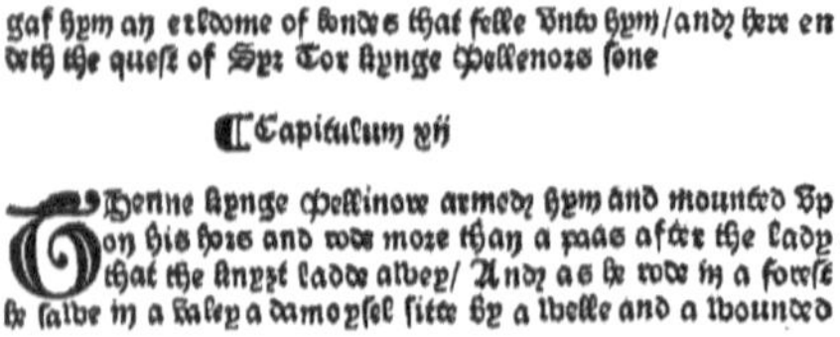

gaf hym an erldome of londes that felle Vnto hym/andr there en
wth the quest of Syr Tor kynge Pellenors sone

¶Capitulum xij

Therme kynge Pellinore armedr hym and mounted Vp
on his hors and rode more than a paas after the Lady
that the knyzt ladde awey/ Andr as he rode in a forest
he salwe in a Valey a damoysel sitte By a welle and a wounded

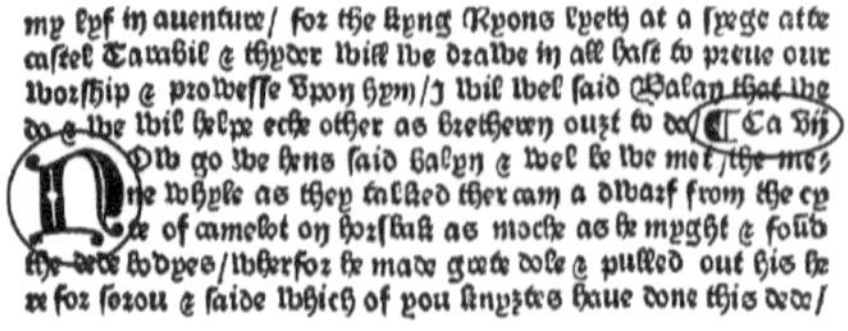

my lyf in auenture/ for the kyng Ryons lyeth at a syege atte
castel Tawbil & thyder wil be drawe in all hast to preue our
worship & prowesse Vpon hym/J wil wel said Balan that we
do & the wil helpe eche other as Brethern ouzt to do ¶Ca Vij
Now go we hens said Balyn & wel be we met/the mene
whyle as they talked ther cam a dwarf from the cy
te of camelot on horsbak as moche as he myght & found
the dede bodyes/wherfor he made grete dole & pulled out his he
re for sorou & saide Which of you knyztes haue done this dede/

Caxton, there are 27 pages with intralinear chapter divisions, and as many as 23 of these divisions occur where Winchester has no coloured initial letters.[3] Three of these divisions cannot be compared with an equivalent passage in Winchester, because the latter lacks its first and last quires. That is to say, in most of the places where the Caxton has intralinear chapter divisions, Caxton's setting-copy apparently did not have any heavier divisional mark than *virgula suspensiva* in double form (//).

What happened in these pages will be that, first, Caxton wrote the marks for the chapter divisions in his setting-copy. Then, his foreman must be supposed to have cast off the pages with 35 lines of text so as to allow a line for the chapter division indicator and two blank lines around it. The editorial marks for the chapter division, however, seem not have been very clear to the person who cast off the text. He sometimes overlooked the division mark, failed to allow the necessary lines for a chapter division, and mis-estimated the amount of the text. Thus, at least part of the cause of the mis-estimation for these pages during the casting-off process resided in Caxton's insufficiently conspicuous instructions for the chapter divisions.

Tsuyoshi Mukai's study of Wynkyn de Worde's *Morte Darthur* also suggests that Caxton's instructions for the chapter divisions were inconspicuous. It has been believed that de Worde used the Caxton as his base text for the *Morte Darthur*. However, Mukai collated Winchester, the Caxton and de Worde's 1498 edition, and found that the readings of de Worde agree closely with Winchester against the Caxton in Caxton's Book 18, Chapters 20 and 21. These chapters consist of precisely four pages, Y4 and Y5 of the Caxton. From these, Mukai came to the conclusion that de Worde used Caxton's setting-copy in the pages concerned, because Y4 and Y5 of Caxton's edition,

---

[3] Sig. cc3r, which has only 37 lines of the text, is not under consideration here, as this intralinear chapter division is unlikely to be the result of a compositor's effort to adjust the badly cast-off text. Sig. y2r, the only example where the intralinear chapter division corresponds to a coloured initial letter in Winchester, will be discussed in the following section.

which de Worde adopted as his base text, might have been stained and illegible, or might have been missing. In either case, de Worde departed from Caxton's edition in these four pages, and turned to Caxton's setting-copy. Interestingly, de Worde failed to divide the text at Book 18 Chapter 21, and consequently he produced 'a three-page long "run-on" text'.[4] This is very unusual for de Worde, who corrected his master's mistakes of chapter numbering elsewhere. This shows that the instruction for Chapter 21 in Caxton's setting-copy as de Worde's 'back-up' text was so inconspicuous that de Worde and his workers overlooked it.

The following survey of missing chapter numbers in the Caxton also supports the view that Caxton's editorial marks for the chapter divisions were not very clear. Missing chapter numbers in the Caxton have been entirely neglected by scholars, except for N. F. Blake's discussion of the features of Caxton's table of contents:

> Caxton then set about making a table of contents. As we have seen, in the text itself the chapters were indicated simply by a number; no heading was provided. But for a table of contents more was needed. So the text had to be gone through to provide a suitable heading which was then entered into the table of contents. This labour was performed after the book was in print, for during its course various errors were discovered. These were chiefly a failure to include all numbers in the sequence of chapter numbering. Book 1 lacks chapters 4, 5 and 26, book 4 chapter 19, book 7 chapter [25],[5] and so on. The compiler added the missing numbers to the previous one in his table so that we get entries like:

> > How syr Marhaws justed with syr Gawayn & syr Ewayn and overthrewe them bothe. capitulo xviii and xix

> He forgot, however, to do this for 1. 26. [. . .] That these errors which were discovered in the text during the compilation of the table were not corrected is itself sufficient proof that the text was already in print.[6]

---

[4] Tsuyoshi Mukai, 'De Worde's 1498 *Morte Darthur* and Caxton's Copy-Text', *Review of English Studies*, n.s. 51 (2000), 24–40 (pp. 30–34).

[5] The text itself lacks chapter 25, not chapter 26 as Blake says. Blake says so presumably because Caxton's table of contents gives number 25 together with 26, thus it reads: 'How the quene of Orkeney came to this feste of pentecoste / & sir gawayn & his brethern cam to aske hir blessyng xxv xxvj'. In this case, the compiler has added the missing number to the 'following' one in his table, and not to the 'previous' one.

[6] N. F. Blake, 'Caxton Prepares his Edition of the *Morte Darthur*', in *William Caxton and English Literary Culture*, ed. by N. F. Blake (London: Hambledon, 1991), pp. 199–211 (pp. 210–11).

Blake's view of missing chapter numbers, however, needs to be reconsidered. As to Book 1 Chapter 26 (Figure 8) and Book 7 Chapter 25 (Figure 9), Blake's explanation that the errors were 'chiefly a failure to include all numbers in the sequence of chapter numbering' might be proper.

As can be seen in Figure 8, in Book 1, though Chapter 25 starts in c3v, the next division (on c4v) is numbered 27: thus, there is no Chapter 26.

Figure 8: Caxton's mis-numbering of a chapter (Book 1 Chapter 26).

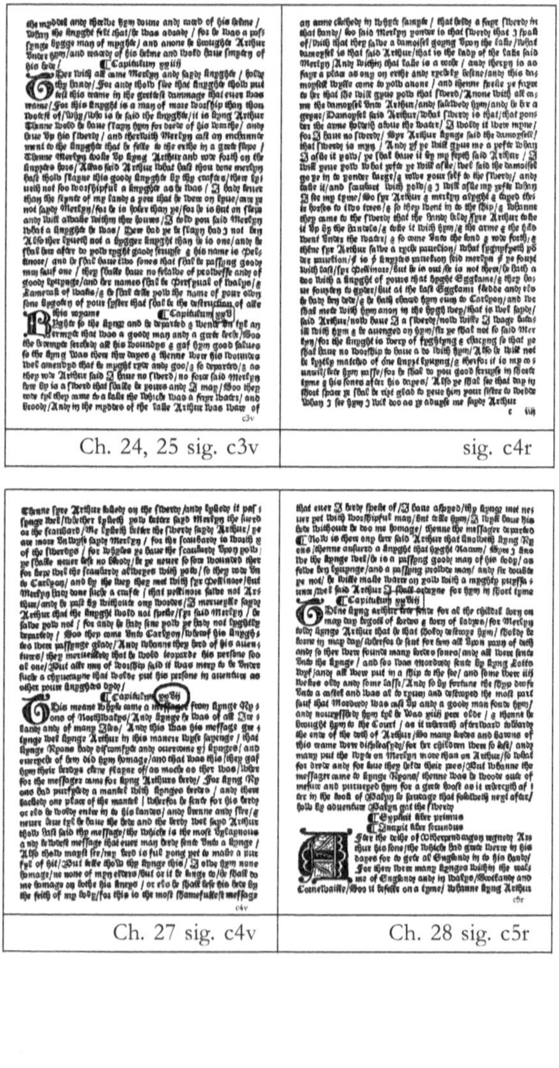

Ch. 24, 25 sig. c3v

sig. c4r

Ch. 27 sig. c4v

Ch. 28 sig. c5r

Figure 9: Caxton's mis-numbering of a chapter (Book 7 Chapter 25).

Ch. 24 sig. o5r	Ch. 26 sig. o5v	Ch. 27 sig. o6r

Consequently, the following chapter is also wrongly numbered. When Caxton composed the table of contents, he just followed his text; since Chapter 26 did not exist in the text, he did not include Chapter 26 in his table of contents:

How Arthur by the meane of Merlyn gate Excalybur hys swerde of the lady of the lake   Capitulo xxv

How tydynges cam to arthur that kyng ryons had ouercome xj kynges & how he desyred arthu[r]s berde to purfyl his mantel   Capitulo xxvij [.][7]

As the heading of the table of contents explains, Book 1 Chapter 25 starts with the episode in which King Arthur gets a sword from the Lady of the Lake by the help of Merlin. On their way back to Carlion, Merlin reveals that the scabbard is more important than the sword, and this chapter finishes when King Arthur and Merlin go back to Carlion. The story in this chapter is so coherent that it is most natural to consider that there was no Chapter 26 from the beginning.

In Book 7 (Figure 9), the division after Chapter 24 is numbered 26, and thus there is no Chapter 25. In his table of contents, Caxton treated this

---

[7]   *Sir Thomas Malory, 'Le Morte D'Arthur', Printed by William Caxton 1485: Facsimile*, intro. by Paul Needham (London: Scolar Press, 1976), sig. 1 π 5r.

mistake differently from the previous example, and added the missing number '25' to the following one:

> How kyng Arthur pardoned them / and demaunded of them where syr Gareth was   Capitulo xxiiij
>
> How the quene of Orkeney came to this feste of pentecoste / & sir gawayn & his brethern cam to aske hir blessyng   xxv xxvj [.][8]

Chapter 26 starts with arrival of Queen of Orkney, and comprises basically the conversation between King Arthur and her. Here again, it is difficult to assume that a chapter division was somehow squeezed out from the text, because the story is coherent. It is more natural to consider that Caxton simply mis-numbered the chapter divisions.

Three of the missing chapter divisions (Book 1, Chapters 4 and 5 in Figure 10, and Book 4, Chapter 19 in Figure 11), however, seem not to have been caused by simple mis-numbering. As Figure 10 clearly shows, Book 1 Chapter 3 is far too long to be regarded as a single chapter. Chapter 3, which begins in a2v, continues without break, for 3 pages and 37 lines, to a4v where Chapter 6 starts, thus, the chapter numbers jump from 3 to 6. As the average length of one chapter is a page and a half, it seems reasonable to consider that Caxton originally intended to make divisions for Chapters 4 and 5. The chapter heading in the table of contents clearly shows that Caxton regarded that single chapter as three stories:

> Of the byrthe of kyng arthur and of his nouryture / & of the deth of kyng vtherpendragon / and how Arthur was chosen kyng and of wondres and meruaylles of a swerde taken out of a stone by the sayd Arthur capitulo iij iiij & v [.][9]

The same can be said of the missing chapter division seen in Book 4 (Figure 11). Chapter 18 begins in g6r and continues, for two pages and 35 lines, to g7v where Chapter 20 starts. This text is certainly long enough to comprise two chapters. Malory often makes reference to his 'books', and interestingly enough, Caxton sometimes seems to have taken this kind of reference as a landmark of Malory's change of topics.[10] Thus, one can speculate that Caxton

---

[8]   The Caxton, sig. 1 π 8r–8v.

[9]   The Caxton, sig. 1 π 4v.

[10]   According to Tomomi Kato's *Concordance to 'The Works of Sir Thomas Malory'* (Tokyo: University of Tokyo Press, 1974), out of Malory's 71 references to his books, 19 appear near Caxton's textual divisions. As many as 13 of these divisions do not accord to Winchester's coloured initial letters, thus they had to be clearly invented by Caxton himself.

Figure 10: Missing chapters in Caxton's Morte *(Book 1, Chapters 4 and 5).*

Ch. 3 sig. a2v	(Ch. 4) sig. a3r	(Ch. 5) sig. a3v

From Ch. 3 to Ch. 6:
3 pages and 37 lines.

sig. a4r	Ch. 6 sig. a4v

intended to create the division between Chapter 18 and 19 right after the reference to the book, which is emphasised in Figure 11:

> As the book reherceth in frensshe ther were many knyghtes that ouermatched syr gawayne for alle the thryes myghte that he had /Syr Launcelot de lake /syr Trystrams / syr Bors de ganys /syr Percyuale /syr Pellias & syr Marhaus /these six kny3tes had the better of sir gawayn [.][11]

---

[11] The Caxton, sig. g7r.

Figure 11: Missing chapter in Caxton's Morte *(Book 4, Chapter 19).*

Ch. 18 sig. g6r	sig. g6v
(Ch. 19) sig. g7r	Ch. 20 sig. g7v

From Ch. 18 to Ch. 20:
2 pages and 35 lines.

In the table of contents, it is said that the content of Chapter 18 and 19 is 'How syr Marhaws Justed with syr Gawayn & syr Ewayn and ouerthrewe them bothe'.[12] The joust, however, finishes just before the reference to the

---

[12] The Caxton, sig. 1 π 6v.

Figure 12: Missing chapter in Caxton's Morte *(Book 9, Chapter 43).*

Ch. 42 sig. &3v	(Ch. 43) sig. &4r	Ch. 44 sig. &4v

book, and the rest describes how Marhalt, Gawain and Ywain went to Marhalt's place, and how they all departed to seek adventures after they healed their wounds. It is reasonable to conclude that although Caxton originally intended to divide the text into Chapter 18 and 19, some physical aspect of Chapter 19 squeezed the chapter division out of the text.

Although Book 9 Chapter 43 is missing from the text (Figure 12), it is restored in Caxton's table of contents:

The heading for chapter 43 corresponds to the paragraph that starts at the middle of &4r. The setting-copy itself probably has had a paragraph mark

---

[13]   The Caxton, sig. 2 π 3r. I would like to thank Miss Satoko Tokunaga for drawing my attention to this missing chapter division.

or a *virgula suspensiva* in a double form in this particular place, and Caxton, in the margin, instructed his compositor to create a chapter division. Although the compositor overlooked Caxton's instruction, he acted on whatever mark stood in his setting-copy and inserted a paraph and a white space. When Caxton made a table of contents after the text was printed, he did not combine Chapters 42 and 43, probably because there was a paraph and a white space for Chapter 43. He may have considered that it would be easy for a reader to notice the textual break for Chapter 43, and thus gave the heading of Chapter 43 in his table of contents.

From these pieces of evidence alone, it is reasonable to conclude that Caxton's setting-copy originally did not have divisions in these particular places. Caxton must have written inconspicuous editorial marks in his setting-copy when he first read through the text, causing mis-estimations in the casting-off process, i.e., when he or a foreman looked over the text for the second time.

The fact that some chapter divisions are wrongly numbered by compositors also seems to suggest that Caxton's editorial marks for chapter divisions were sometimes unclear.[14] Although there is no basis for a comparison in Book 1, as Winchester lacks its first quire, the hypothetical Chapter 19 in Book 4 (Figure 11) and Book 9 Chapter 43 (Figure 12) correspond to mere double slashes in Winchester. In these places, the intermediate text Y and the archetype X most probably did not have any clear divisions, and Caxton invented these divisions. However, because his marks were not conspicuous, the same kind of mistake occurred as with the intralinear chapter divisions. Whoever cast off the text must have overlooked the divisional mark, failed to take the necessary lines for a chapter division into account, and mis-estimated the amount of the text. Figure 7 on p. 50 shows that intralinear chapter division needs only half a line. If the compositors had noticed the marks for these

---

[14] Compositors seem to have mistaken Book 7, Chapters 21 for 22, 34 for 24; Book 8 Chapters 21 for 22, 29 for 19; Book 9, Chapters 18 for 13, 23 for 13, 27 for 17, 29 for 19; Book 10 Chapters 27 for 17, 28 for 18, 47 for 44, 70 for 72; Book 18, Chapters 22 for 20, 23 for 22; Book 20 Chapter 15 for 14.

There is another kind of mistake with chapter divisions: a compositor who type-set the table of contents somehow skipped over chapter headings. The heading of Book 1 Chapter 16 does not exist in the table of contents. Book 9 Chapter 13 of the text is wrongly numbered 14 in the table of contents, and thus the heading of Chapter 14 does not exist in the table of contents. Another irregular chapter heading is Book 10 Chapters 83 and 84 (wrongly numbered 68). Although both chapters exist in the text, chapter headings for these two chapters are combined into one: 'How syr palomydes brouȝt to syr epynogris his lady / & how sir palomydes & syr safer were assaylled ca lxxxiij & lxxiiij' (The Caxton, sig. 2 π 5r).

chapter divisions, they could have squeezed the chapter divisions into the text by using ampersands and by deleting some words. This did not happen to Book 1 Chapters 4 and 5, Book 4 Chapter 19, and Book 9 Chapter 43, because the editorial marks for these chapters were so inconspicuous that they escaped the notice of not only whoever cast off the text but also of the compositors, with the result that these chapter divisions are missing in the Caxton.

The converse probably happened in <type B-6+> pages, the pages with excessive paraphs. Recognising the editorial marks for chapter divisions, a foreman usually would cast off pages determined as needing chapter divisions with only 35 lines of text. Because the editorial markings for chapter divisions were not very clear, whoever cast off the text might have sometimes shortened the text of the setting-copy as was his habit, when actually shortening had not been asked for. Thus, both pages with chapter divisions and <type B-6+> pages seem to have been cast off with only 35 lines of text on average. In other words, in <type B-6+> pages, the length of the omissions being subtracted from the length of the surplus parts becomes very close to the number of lines necessary for chapter divisions; as the numbers below the signature numbers in Table 3 indicate, the minimum difference is 1.52 lines, the maximum is 8.29 lines, and the average difference is 3.43 lines.[15] These numbers 1.5, 8.3 and 3.4 are close to the numbers which represent the lowest, the highest and the average number of lines used when dividing chapters: 0, 5 and 3.[16] The setting-copy, which we had assumed for the sake of argument was very like Winchester, was cast off only in 35 lines, which corresponds to both pages with excessive paraphs and pages with a chapter division. This strongly suggests that, during the casting-off process, a foreman who was in the habit of casting off shorter pages for chapter divisions inadvertently shortened the setting-copy's text on the pages which correspond to <type B-6+> pages in Caxton's book. This mistake is all the more likely because the pages including chapter divisions comprise as much as 60 % of the entire book, and because all the pages preceding and succeeding <B-6+> pages contain chapter divisions.

Thus it becomes clear that mistakes happened during the casting-off process of the *Morte* due to unclear editorial marks for chapter divisions, so that the compositors were forced to use every possible device in order to make the page divisions flow seamlessly. The compositor whose misfortune it was to have to type-set <type B-6+> pages recognised the mistakes, and supposing that his alterations would not change the fundamental meaning

---

[15] See pp. 35–36 above.
[16] See Table 4, p. 44 above.

of the text, inserted paraphs and white spaces, and added words in order to lengthen the amount of printing. Paraphs in Caxton's *Morte* therefore play two roles: first, to punctuate the text following the scribal convention; but secondly, to increase the apparent amount of text, so that the badly cast-off text would be able to fill the required 38 lines.

As Caxton's markings for chapter divisions were inconspicuous, whoever cast off the text seems to have had trouble taking the necessary lines for chapter divisions into account correctly. Sometimes this person did not recognise the editorial marks, failed to cast off the text of the setting-copy short, and consequently, forced the compositors to type-set intralinear chapter divisions. At other times, the text of the setting-copy was unnecessarily shortened by the habit of casting off pages for chapter divisions, and the compositors were forced to type-set <type B-6+> pages.

2. Caxton's Irregular Setting-Copy

The inconspicuous editorial hand for chapter divisions in Caxton's setting-copy suggests that the setting-copy may very well have been irregular and messy. Gaskell discusses the nature of setting-copies used by early printers:

> Manuscript copy, as printers often complained, might be an ill-written author's draft much blotted and corrected, but it seems that a good many manuscripts intended for the printer were fair-copied, either by the author or by a professional scribe. Hornschuch, in his correctors' manual of 1608 implied that it was normal for vernacular manuscripts to be fair-copied for the printer, adding that the scribes who did it cared more for calligraphic elegance than for the accuracy of the text.[17]

Indeed, Caxton's only surviving setting-copy, that for the *Nova rhetorica*, is rather fairly written. There is a reason to believe that the author, Traversanus, wrote the *Nova rhetorica* with the intention of letting the work be printed from the outset.[18]

---

[17] Philip Gaskell, *A New Introduction to Bibliography: The Classic Manual of Bibliography* (1972; repr. Winchester: St Paul's Bibliographies; New Castle, DE: Oak Knoll Press, 1995), p. 40.

[18] Traversanus was a learned Franciscan friar, who travelled in Italy, Austria, France, Flanders, and also England. The *Nova rhetorica* was written in Cambridge, and it is considered that Caxton was asked to publish it by the author, who brought his own copy. See Lotte Hellinga, *Caxton in Focus: The Beginning of Printing in England* (London: British Library, 1982), p. 46; Blake, *Caxton and his World* (London: Deutsch, 1969), pp. 196–97; George D. Painter,

Table 8: Number of paraphs in a page.

	1 paraph in a page	2	3	4	5	6 or more
Morte	213 pages	122	38	25	14	11
Troy	Only '¶ How . . . '					
Jason	17	3	1			
Siege	Only '¶ How . . . '					
Eneydos	24	5	1	1		

The setting-copies of Caxton's own translations would also probably be tidy fair copies. As Caxton was an exceptionally busy printer who did not have time for unnecessary repetition, it would be natural for him to have prepared a text for printing while he was translating it as far as he could. The setting-copies of Caxton's translations most probably would be his own hand-written manuscripts, and it is reasonable to assume that Caxton did his best to produce his translations in a consistent hand, so that the casting-off process would be easier.

In fact, the layout of a number of prose romances translated by Caxton is very much less irregular than that of the *Morte*. Four of Caxton's romances, the *History of Troy* (1473–74) with 352 leaves, *Jason* (1477) with 150 leaves, the *Siege of Jerusalem* (1481) with 144 leaves and *Eneydos* (1490) with 86 leaves are compared with the *Morte Darthur* in Table 8.[19]

Table 8 reveals that it was only in Caxton's print of the *Morte* that paraphs were used excessively in a page. In all the romances, the paraphs are used in order to indicate the beginning of new chapters; Caxton gives a paraph first, and then briefly explains the content of the next chapter, such as 'How . . .'. In *Troy* and the *Siege*, the paraphs are used only in this way. The others also contain the paraphs as smaller section indicators, but the frequency of

---

William Caxton: A Quincentenary Biography of England's First Printer (London: Chatto & Windus, 1976), pp. 96–97.

[19] Microfilms and a facsimile of these works have been consulted. *Troy*, *STC* 15375 (reel 1209); *Jason*, *STC* 15383 (reel 47); *Siege*, English Experience Series, 604 (New York: Da Capo Press; Amsterdam: Theatrum Orbis Terrarum, 1973); *Eneydos*, *STC* 24796 (reel 17). These works are printed in folio format with a single column. Out of eight prose romances translated by Caxton, *Paris and Vienne* (1485) and *Charles the Great* (1485) are excluded here, because these two works are printed in two columns. Microfilms of two other books, *Blanchardin and Eglantine* (1489–91) and *Four Sons of Aymon* (1489–91) have proved unavailable so far.

paraphs per page in books other than the *Morte* is rather low. In addition, there are no intralinear chapter divisions at all in Caxton's translations.

Thus the layout of Caxton's prose romances makes the irregular layout of the *Morte* stand out. The layout of the *Morte* was different from those setting-copies written by Caxton himself, who must have made them as much of fair copies as he could for the reason we have given. This makes it very unlikely that the setting-copy of the *Morte* was made by Caxton. If Caxton's setting-copy of the *Morte Darthur* caused such a large mis-estimation in the casting off and forced the compositors to create pages such as <type B-6+> and pages with intralinear chapter divisions, it must have been a rough and irregular copy. The fact that the now lost setting-copy of the *Morte* was so defective in these respects suggests that it was not made in Caxton's workshop from the Winchester manuscript, or indeed from any other manuscript either. The *Morte Darthur* is a large volume consisting of more than eight hundred pages. If someone did copy the whole book, this was either for a patron or for a commercial purpose; and in either case, it would have been nothing but a serious job; a seriously copied manuscript for type-setting purposes must have been a rather fair copy, not a messy and irregular copy.[20]

P. J. C. Field compares reconstructed passages from Caxton's setting-copy with the Winchester manuscript in these words:

> A manuscript with a greater number of words per line might have had wider paper, smaller script, more abbreviation, or narrower margins [than the Winchester manuscript]. Any or all of the last three of these would suggest a more workaday product than Winchester.[21]

Thus, in Caxton's workshop, while the *Morte Darthur* was prepared for the press, although Caxton did not say so, there must have been two complete copies of Malory's *Morte Darthur*[22] – an irregular workaday copy which Caxton used as his setting-copy, and the Winchester manuscript.

---

[20] The present writer would like to thank Professor Field for a stimulating discussion in Tokyo on 8 December 1997, which led her to consider this possibility.

[21] P. J. C. Field, 'The Earliest Texts of Malory's *Morte Darthur*', *Poetica*, 38 (1993), 18–31 (p. 30). Field's comparison is based on the reconstructed readings of Caxton's setting-copy by Lotte Hellinga and Toshiyuki Takamiya. See, Hellinga, *Caxton in Focus*, pp. 91–94, Takamiya, 'Editor / Compositor at Work: The Case of Caxton's Malory', in *Arthurian and Other Studies Presented to Shunichi Noguchi*, ed. by Takashi Suzuki and Tsuyoshi Mukai (Cambridge: Brewer, 1993), pp. 143–51 and 'Chapter Divisions and Page Breaks in Caxton's *Morte Darthur*', *Poetica*, 45 (1996), 63–78, passim.

[22] As for the Roman War episode, there existed the third copy, a version which was probably rewritten by Caxton. See pp. 4–5 above. That pages of Caxton's Book 5 have a

3. Shortening Malory's Stemma

In spite of the challenging argument put by Hellinga, Vinaver's collateral stemma is still fundamentally sound and convincing. Many examples where passages correspond to the sources, but not to the other primary text, are found in both Winchester and the Caxton. This can be explained only by a collateral relationship between the two extant texts. However, Vinaver's stemma (Stemma 3) needs to be re-examined in the light of all the new evidence. In fact, the existence of intermediate copies in Vinaver's stemma has been recently opened to question by several scholars. We may naturally ask if Caxton's setting-copy was Malory's own holograph manuscript.

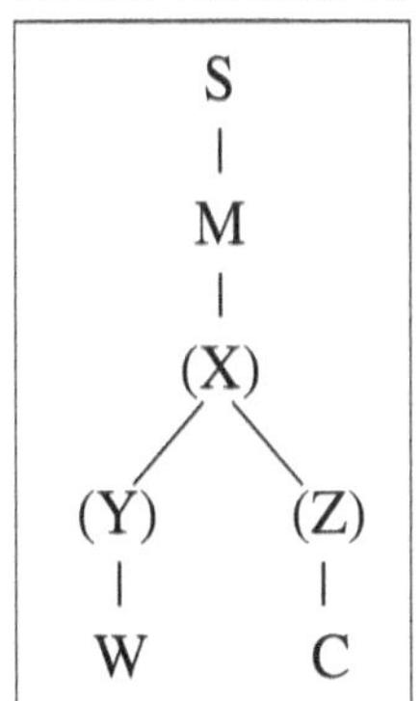

Stemma 3: Vinaver's stemma reconsidered.

The fact established in the present study that many mistakes happened in the casting-off process due to the irregularity of Caxton's setting-copy suggests a copying process that did not have enough money behind it. It is interesting in this respect that Malory himself was obviously short of money as a result of his long experience in prison. Field says that '[p]rison in the Middle Ages was expensive both in itself and because it made it difficult to keep one's income coming in smoothly'.[23] Sir Thomas Malory of Newbold Revel spent nearly eight years in and out of prison, charged with attempted murder, rape, extortion, malicious damage, and sacrilegious robbery.[24] In fact, in his earlier imprisonment, Malory was sued for debt for quite a small sum which he was unable to pay. This relative poverty could well have led to Malory being unable to afford fully professional copies of his own book.

Vinaver believed that 'the incredible story' of Pellam and Balyn lying for days under a heap of the rubble could only have been produced by two consecutive mistakes made by different scribes, and he therefore postulated

---

rather consistent layout – for example, no <type B-6+> pages are found in Book 5 – supports this idea. Caxton may be assumed to have rewritten the episode consistently so that the text could be easily cast off.

[23] P. J. C. Field, *The Life and Times of Sir Thomas Malory*, Arthurian Studies, 29 (Cambridge: Brewer, 1993), p. 108.

[24] P. J. C. Field, 'The Last Years of Sir Thomas Malory', *Bulletin of the John Rylands Library*, 64 (1982), 433–56 (p. 435).

an inserted intermediate copy Z between the archetype X and Caxton's book.[25] That, however, was his only reason for introducing Z into his stemma. Compared to the hundreds of passages which led him to infer a collateral relationship between Winchester and the Caxton, his grounds for believing in the existence of Z were from the beginning quite slim.

Vinaver's theory of copy Z was overturned by Field's re-examination of the passage. Field first criticises Vinaver's criteria of 'the incredible':

> This is a tale of wonder, in which one of the characters named has recently jumped from the top of the tower of a castle into a moat without hurting himself, and the other is about to spend years miraculously suspended between life and death until his wounds are cured by an embrace from the Grail-knight.[26]

Then, Field points out that Vinaver failed to notice two important variants in the following passage:

> W f. 31r: And there with the castell brake rooffe and wallis and felle downe
> C sig. d6r: and therwith the castel roofe and wallys brake and fylle
>
> W: to the erthe And Balyn felle downe and myght nat styrre hande nor foote
> C: to the erthe/ and balyn felle doune so that he myghte not stere foote nor hand/
>
> W: and for the moste party of that castell was **dede** thorow
> C: And so the moost party of the castel that was **falle doune** thorugh
>
> W: the dolorouse stroke // Ryght so lay kynge Pellam and Balyne iij dayes
> C: that dolorous stroke laye vpon Pellam and balyn thre dayes.[27]

The reading of Winchester is certainly correct, *apart from* the punctuation. From the third to the fourth line of Winchester, the passage 'for the moste party of that castell was dede thorow the dolorouse stroke' should function as a subordinate clause of 'ryght so lay kynge Pellam and Balyne three dayes'. However, Winchester includes a *virgula suspensiva* in a double form. As Field explains, if the Winchester reading was a single sentence, it obviously reproduces 'something implied in the source'.[28] Of course, it is impossible to determine

---

[25] See p. 11 above.

[26] Field, 'Earliest Texts ', p. 28.

[27] Lines arranged, and emphases added by the present writer; transcribed from the facsimile of the Caxton and *The Winchester Malory: A Facsimile,* intro. by N. R. Ker, EETS SS 4 (London: Oxford University Press, 1976).

[28] Field, 'Earliest Texts', p. 28.

whether Caxton's setting-copy had the same punctuation as the Winchester manuscript. We can only speculate. However, Caxton's reading seems to be the result of conscious alteration or correction of the sentence. And thus, the second variants, not mentioned by Vinaver, the alteration by Caxton, from 'dede' in Winchester to 'falle doune', can be explained as follows:

> It is much more elegant to assume that the Caxton was rewritten to make sense of what now stands in Winchester, which could have appeared nonsense either because, as punctuated, the first of its two sentences has no main verb, or because someone reading in a hurry took *moste party* to apply to the building rather than to its inhabitants and so saw the participle *dede* as absurd. Someone certainly reworked the passage as one sentence and replaced *dede* with a verb that could apply to a building, *felle downe*, a verb that was probably in his mind because it stood in the previous sentence. The remaining alterations can be seen as an attempt to restore grammatical propriety while keeping as much of the original wording as possible. There is nothing to suggest that this happened in two stages, and it is much more plausible in one. The whole of Vinaver's case for an intermediary between X and C therefore falls.[29]

This raises a possibility that Caxton's setting-copy, the other copy in Caxton's workshop, could be the archetype X in Vinaver's stemma. Field also carefully re-examines the passage which Vinaver regarded as the result of two stages of transmission from the archetype to Winchester. For copy Y, however, he judges 'Vinaver's hypothesis to be the stronger [than the alternative hypothesis that Field had tested], although falling well short of the certainty that might be assumed from his exposition'.[30]

This shortening of Vinaver's stemma can be supported by Yuji Nakao's linguistic evidence. In late fifteenth-century England, the words, 'betwix', 'betwixt' and 'between' were used so interchangeably that both Winchester and the Caxton contain both versions of the spelling. However, there is a 'noticeable fact with regard to the distribution', that 'the majority of instances of {betwixt} in W[inchester] corresponds to {betwix} in [the] C[axton], and {between} in W[inchester] also to {between} in [the] C[axton]'.[31] Nakao gives further examples of language correspondence ('sithen', 'sith', 'sin' and 'sins'; 'afore', 'before', 'tofore', 'aforne', 'beforne' and 'toforne'), and suggests

---

[29] Field, 'Earliest Texts', p. 29.

[30] Field, 'Earliest Texts', p. 27.

[31] Yuji Nakao, 'On the Relationship between the Winchester Malory and Caxton's Malory', in *Arthurian and Other Studies Presented to Shunichi Noguchi*, ed. by Takashi Suzuki and Tsuyoshi Mukai (Cambridge: Brewer, 1993), pp. 201–09 (p. 201).

that Winchester and the Caxton may be 'more closely related to each other than would presumably be the case with two texts of a collateral relation'.[32] Although Nakao's study 'misses the essential difference between Caxton's Malory and the Winchester MS, viz., that the former has a Southern, and the latter a Midland basis, dialectally speaking',[33] it is still significant. These correspondences of interchangeable words obviously cast some doubt on the existence of intermediate texts between Winchester and the Caxton.

Helen Cooper also supports this view. She points out that not only the coloured initial letters, but the double slashes in Winchester agree with Caxton's chapter divisions, then concludes that the text divisions and punctuation of Winchester must derive from a common exemplar underlying both. She then puts the system of text-divisions within reach of Malory himself. Cooper further proposes that the rubricated names and the system of abbreviation of Merlin as M may have been features of the exemplar of Winchester. These possibilities suggest that it is desirable to shorten the stemma between Malory and extant texts as much as possible.[34]

There has even been some discussion of the idea that the archetype from which Winchester and the Caxton descend was Malory's original version.[35] Richard R. Griffith points out that Caxton printed his book 'after a copye unto me delyverd, whyche copye syr Thomas Malorye dyd take oute of certeyn bookes of Frensshe and reduced it into Englysshe'.[36] Although 'this may be too literal a reading of the printer's words', Griffith goes on to say, 'Caxton's sprawling sentence describing the circumstances of his publication of the *Morte* [. . .] actually asserts that he used the author's own manuscript'.[37]

Vinaver's arguments in support of copy X, however, are still irrefutable.

---

[32] Nakao, 'On the Relationship between the Winchester Malory and Caxton's Malory', p. 201.

[33] Jeremy J. Smith, 'Some Spellings in Caxton's Malory', *Poetica*, 24 (1986), 58–63 (p. 60, n. 9).

[34] For the system of abbreviation in Winchester, see Helen Cooper, 'M for Merlin: The Case of the Winchester Manuscript', in *Medieval Heritage: Essays in Honour of Tadahiro Ikegami*, ed. by Masahiko Kanno and others (Tokyo: Yushodo, 1997), pp. 93–107; for the textual divisions, see her 'Opening up the Malory Manuscript', in *The Malory Debate: Essays on the Texts of 'Le Morte Darthur'*, ed. by Bonnie Wheeler, Robert L. Kindrick and Michael N. Salda, Arthurian Studies, 47 (Cambridge: Brewer, 2000), pp. 255–84.

[35] N. F. Blake, 'Caxton at Work: A Reconsideration', in *The Malory Debate*, pp. 233–53.

[36] *Works*, p. cxlv.

[37] Richard R. Griffith, 'Caxton's Copy-Text for *Le Morte Darthur*: Tracing the Provenance', in *Traditions and Innovations: Essays on British Literature of the Middle Ages and the Renaissance*, ed. by David G. Allen and Robert A. White (Newark: University of Delaware Press, 1990), pp. 75–87 (pp. 76–77).

Vinaver claims in his Introduction that the archetype could not be Malory's holograph copy because the archetype contained the errors mistaking the final 't' for 'e', and 'e' for 't'.[38] In a fifteenth century hand, 't' is completely different from 'e', and it is very unlikely that the author who had intended to write 'e' erroneously wrote 't', or vice versa. Field also recently claims to have identified errors in the archetype of a kind that only a scribe would make.[39] If these claims are borne out by future scholarly investigation, we have to accept that Caxton did not set his *Morte Darthur* from Malory's first holograph copy. It is not unusual, however, in any period for an author to make a fair copy of his work from original drafts that may be disfigured with alterations and afterthoughts, or to have such a copy made for him – the best copy that he can afford. In such a situation, an author may make typical 'scribal' errors that he would not make in the course of composition, because time separated him from the words he originally wrote. As Malory completed his work sometime between 4 March 1469 and 3 March 1470, and died on 14 March 1471, he hardly had had time both to write the *Morte Darthur* in a draft form and to fair-copy it himself.[40] These conditions, however, would not affect a copy made for him, which have been made from Malory's pages as he was writing them.

To sum up, it is now clear that Caxton's irregular use of paraphs and irregular layout of chapter divisions were a result of compositors' efforts to adjust the badly cast-off text into a page of 38 lines. The current study has also revealed an interesting aspect of Caxton's setting-copy: the editorial marks for the chapter divisions sometimes seem to have been inconspicuous, and the most plausible explanation for this is the strikingly irregular and untidy nature of the setting-copy. We may postulate Malory commissioning the best copy to his book that he could afford, a copy that might very well be below the level of professionalism that the best fifteenth-century English scriptoria could produce for a more affluent patron. The author-patron's relative poverty might have compelled him to employ a copyist who would only write in a cheap and slipshod hand, or to use paper or parchment that was not all uniform in size and shape. The last factor alone could explain much of Caxton's difficulty in casting off his setting-copy.

[38] See p. 10 above.

[39] Field, 'Earliest Texts', p. 29; Field, 'Balin and the Dolorous Stroke', *"A Ful Noble Knyght": A Medieval Newsletter Devoted to the Life and Art of Sir Thomas Malory*, 1.2 (1999), 1–3 (p. 3).

[40] The time Malory himself had available to fair-copy his work might be greater than is currently thought if a discovery of a new document announced by Anne F. Sutton stands scrutiny. See her 'Malory in Newgate: A New Document', *Library*, 7th ser. 1 (2000), 243–62.

4. Caxton's Use of the Winchester Manuscript

Now, the last question remains – how was the Winchester manuscript used in Caxton's workshop? The fact that the traces of printer's ink spread over whole length of the manuscript, from fol. 9r to fol. 433r, strongly suggests that the manuscript was used consistently.[41] Since the setting-copy was irregular and untidy, it is easy to speculate that Winchester was used to decipher the difficult passages in the setting-copy, or when the setting-copy lacked some pages or parts of pages, a practice which was common among the early printers.

Caxton's words in the preface to the *Morte Darthur* are worth reconsideration here. His approach to the work is explained in four different ways: (1) 'I have [. . .] enprysed to **enprynte** a book of the noble hystoryes of the sayd kynge Arthur and of certeyn of his knyghtes, **after a copye** unto me delyverd'; (2) 'I, **accordyng to my copye**, have doon **sette it in enprynte**'; (3) 'I [. . .] present thys book folowyng whyche I have **enprysed t'enprynte**'; and lastly, 'I have **devyded** it into twenty-one bookes, and every book chapytred'.[42] Regarding the editorial procedure, Caxton claimed that he was responsible only for creating the book and chapter divisions.

Even if Caxton's setting-copy were not a rough and irregular draft possibly produced for an impoverished author, we could be sure that it was not divided into books and chapters: after all, Caxton told his readers that he had introduced those divisions himself, and we have seen something of the practical reasons why it was to his advantage to do so. In the Winchester manuscript, on the other hand, there are 111 coloured initial letters, and it is reasonable to suppose there were several in the pages now missing. Two of them are five-line letters with ornament (the *H* on f. 71r and the *S* on f. 409v). A 3-line *A* on f. 349r is also ornamented. Three examples of *I*, on ff. 35r, 113v and 449r, are found outside the written space. Four other initial letters follow 'Explicit . . .' or 'Here endeth . . .', and spaces are left between the lines (ff. 45r, 96r, 148v and 187r). These initials all correspond to the beginnings of Caxton's new books. All other initials are plain red two- or three-line letters, and apart from the second, eighth and ninth initials in the Roman War episode, which Caxton seems to have rewritten with a great

---

[41] Lotte Hellinga, 'The Malory Manuscript and Caxton', in *Aspects of Malory*, ed. by Toshiyuki Takamiya and Derek Brewer, Arthurian Studies, 1 (Cambridge: Brewer, 1981), pp. 127–41 and 220–21 (p. 220, n. 7).

[42] Emphases added; *Works*, pp. cxlv–xlvi.

number of alterations, all initials correspond either to the book or chapter divisions of Caxton's book.

Furthermore, Takagi's collation of the layout of the two versions reveals that out of 374 chapter divisions in Caxton's text which do not correspond to the coloured initial letters in Winchester, more than half correspond either to the beginning of lines or to the *virgula suspensiva* in a double form (//) in the Winchester text (44 and 170 places respectively).[43]

Most of the red initial letters in Winchester coincide with Caxton's book and chapter divisions, and it has been thought that the simplest explanation of this is that both the chapters in the Caxton and the divisions in Winchester were prompted by some features in their archetype. However, the following study of textual divisions in the Caxton and Winchester suggests that some divisions in the Caxton did not exist in the archetype X, nor in the intermediate text Y.

As suggested in the previous section, it was Caxton's inconspicuous editorial marks in his setting-copy that caused intralinear chapter divisions and missing chapter divisions. His inconspicuous editorial markings seem also to have affected the anomalous intralinear chapter division, y2r in Figure 13 (p. 70).

Since Book 9, Chapter 23 in y2r corresponds to the Winchester initial letter 'A', the natural assumption, according to the present scholarly consensus about the text, would be that this division was inherited from the archetype. However, if the archetype itself carried a division in this particular place, there is no obvious reason why Caxton's mark indicating a chapter-break at that point should have been so inconspicuous that whoever cast off the copy overlooked it. This page of the Caxton, moreover, does not exhibit any significant textual variation from Winchester. In other words, we cannot find any explanation for the mis-estimation in y2r other than the chapter division itself. Caxton's inconspicuous editorial hand also explains the reason for the compositor's mistaking Chapter 23 for 13.

From these things, it is reasonable to conclude that Caxton's setting-copy, the archetype, did not have a division in this particular place. Caxton must have written an inconspicuous editorial mark in his setting-copy causing a mis-estimation in the casting-off process. Although it accords with

---

[43] Masako Takagi, 'Rubricated Letters in the Winchester Manuscript and Caxton's Textual Divisions', *Round Table*, 12 (1997), 1–65 [in Japanese]. Because Caxton seems to have rewritten the Roman War episode, the chapter divisions in Book 5 are left out of consideration. Missing chapter divisions discussed above are also excluded here.

Figure 13: Caxton's intralinear chapter division which accords with Winchester's initial letter (Caxton's Book 9, Chapter 23 (sig. y2r), and Winchester's 'A' (f. 207r)).

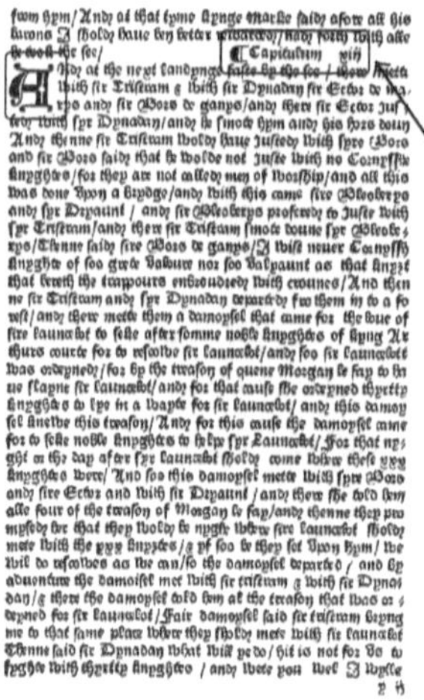

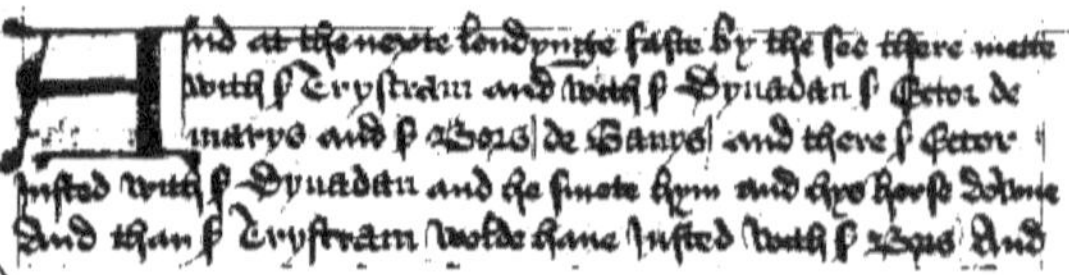

The compositor mistook Ch. 23 for Ch. 13.

Winchester's red initial letter 'A', Caxton's Book 9 Chapter 23 in y2r was not inherited from the archetype.

There are other divisions where the two texts agree which also seem not to have been inherited from the archetype. On f. 22r of Winchester, which is illustrated in Figure 14, the text reads, 'as hit rehersith aftir in the booke of Balyne le Saueage that folowith nexte aftir that was the adventure how Balyne gate þe swerde aft*ir*', then a new section starts with 'Afftir the deth of Vther regned Arthure hys son which [. . .]'.[44] The last word of the previous section ('aftir') belongs to the next section. Vinaver says: '[i]n the copy used by the scribe of W[inchester] this was probably the end of a page, and *after* was inserted as a catchword'.[45] However, Scribe A, who copied these pages, had already written catchwords for himself at the end of f. 16v and presumably at the end of the missing first quire f. 8v. He clearly knew the function of catchwords. It is difficult to believe that Scribe A made a mistake such as inserting the catchword of his exemplar in the text. Moreover, the fact that Scribe B did not at first know the role of catchwords suggests that their exemplar did not have catchwords. Scribe B wrote catchwords on ff. 52v, 60v, 68v, and 340v, but at first did not repeat the words on ff. 53r, 61r, 69r,

---

[44] Winchester, f. 22r.

[45] *Works*, p. 56, n. 6–7.

Figure 14: An initial letter in Winchester not inherited from archetype X (Winchester's 'A' (f. 22r) and Caxton's Book 2, Chapter 1 (sig. c5r)).

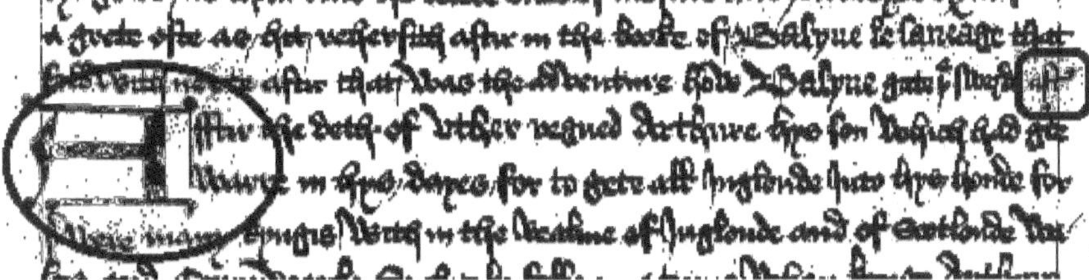

and 341r. It seems to be more probable that here the text in the exemplar was written without any break, and it was the Winchester editor who indicated that the text should be divided at that point. The editor could be one of the scribes, most probably Scribe A.

It was indeed in the scriptoria that the convention of dividing a script fully developed. This tradition of dividing a text at will was also kept by the fifteenth-century scribes who worked on vernacular texts. For example, Doyle and Parkes demonstrate the scribes' division of the *Canterbury Tales* into chapters.[46] The Winchester scribes would naturally have felt free to divide and arrange the text of Malory. Although Vinaver believed that

---

[46] A. I. Doyle and M. B. Parkes, 'The Production of Copies of the *Canterbury Tales* and the *Confessio Amantis* in the Early Fifteenth Century', in *Medieval Scribes, Manuscripts and Libraries: Essays Presented to N. R. Ker*, ed. by M. B. Parkes and Andrew G. Watson (London: Scolar Press, 1978), pp. 163–210 (p. 193).

Winchester has been affected only by mechanical errors, it seems that the scribes also consciously 'edited' the text of Malory, at least by dividing it up. Here, the Winchester scribe first failed to recognise the instruction for a textual division, and wrote what he read in the exemplar.

There is another example similar to the previous one which Vinaver does not mention in his edition. In f. 64v of Winchester, just before the red initial letter, words 'and there' are crossed out (Figure 15). The only reasonable explanation for this error is that the scribe copied 'ye shall nat fayle to haue þᵉ love of hir and there' without any break, and then realised that 'A' in 'and' should be written in a red initial letter. He crossed out the words, 'and there', then started his new section with the initial letter, 'A'. This kind of error could have hardly happened if the exemplar, Y, had a division as clear as the one in Winchester. The text in the exemplar must have been written without any break, and it must have been the Winchester editor who indicated that the text should be divided at that point. The Winchester scribe first failed to recognise the instruction, and wrote what stood in the exemplar. As Winchester's exemplar Y did not have any division in this particular place, we can safely conclude that the archetype did not have a division in this place.

Nevertheless, these divisions in Winchester agree with book and chapter divisions in the Caxton. The chapter division in the Caxton discussed in Figure 13 also agrees with the red initial letter in Winchester. Although these three chapters in the Caxton correspond to Winchester's divisions, it is unlikely that the intermediate copy Y and the archetype in the stemma carried textual divisions in these particular places. Therefore, Caxton did not learn where to divide the text from his setting-copy. Where then did he get these divisions?

When dividing such a long text as the *Morte Darthur*, it would have been very natural for Caxton to consult the Winchester manuscript, since he had it at hand. If the suggestion offered here is true, then even other divisions where the two texts agree may sometimes not have been inherited from their archetype. The agreements of textual divisions between the two texts might have been caused because Winchester influenced Caxton's setting-copy.

Following Hellinga's discoveries, scholars have pointed out the possibility of the Caxton version having been influenced by the Winchester text. However, discussion has usually focused on the readings, not the layout of the text. It is clear that Caxton's setting-copy, the irregular and messy manuscript X, had neither book and chapter divisions nor initial letters. It is most natural to consider that Caxton consulted Winchester, not only when he needed to decipher the irregular writings in the setting-copy, but

Figure 15: An initial letter in Winchester not inherited from archetype X (Winchester's 'A' (f. 64v) and Caxton's Book 4, Chapter 23 (sig. h2r)).

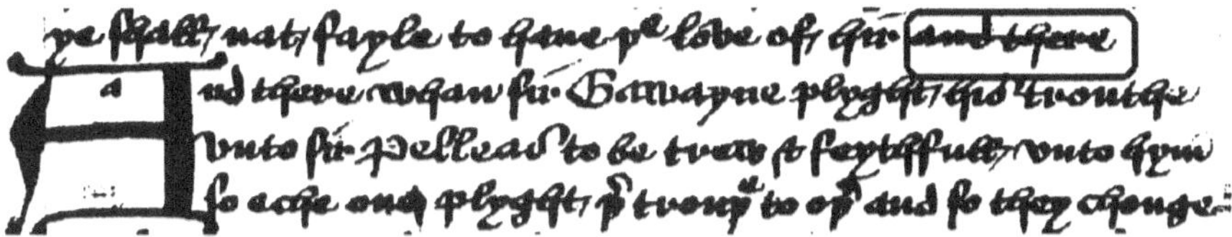

also when he was editing, i.e., dividing the text in the setting-copy.

From this reason, a new stemma for the *Morte Darthur* as illustrated in Stemma 4 is introduced here. With regard to the text outside the Roman War episode, the Caxton and Winchester are in a collateral relationship as Vinaver proposed, though Caxton's setting-copy seems to have been the archetype itself. The Roman War episode seems to have been drastically revised by Caxton, who may have used the *Chronicles of England* as a second source.[47] In the book and chapter divisions of the text, however, the Caxton was a direct lineal descendant of Winchester. In the three examples discussed in this chapter, neither the archetype nor Y had textual divisions. It was the Winchester editor who first decided to divide the text in these places, and wrote instructions in manuscript Y. The Winchester scribes followed those instructions and wrote red initial letters in Winchester. Then, Caxton, while preparing his edition for the *Morte Darthur*, consulted the textual divisions in Winchester, and made them the basis of his division of his 'copye', the archetype, into the books and chapters which were a familiar feature of many later editions until the rediscovery of the Winchester manuscript.

---

[47] See pp. 20–21 above.

Stemma 4: Kato's new stemma.

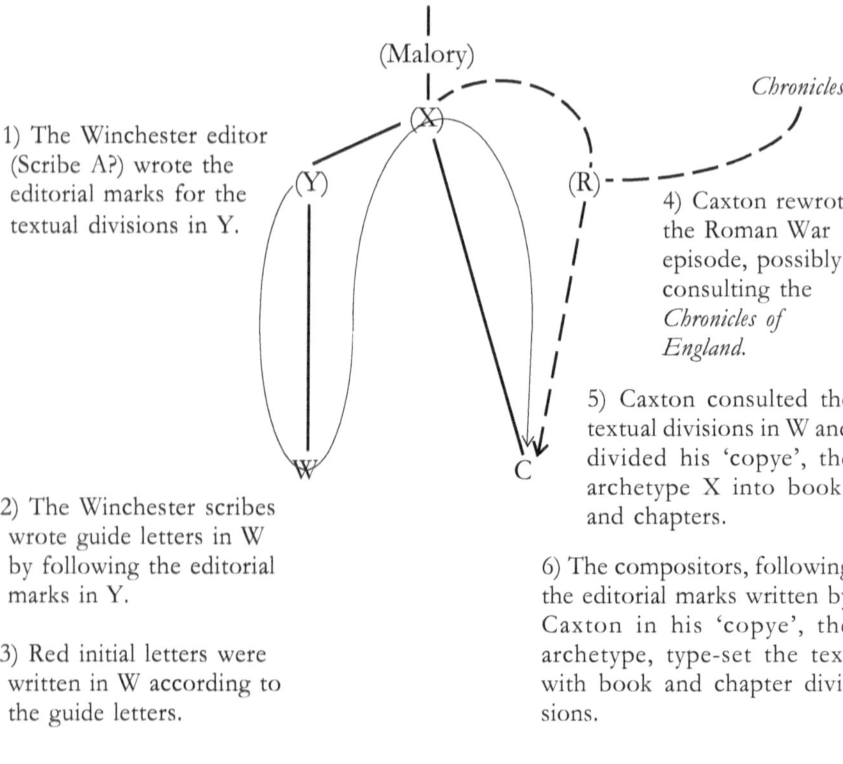

1) The Winchester editor (Scribe A?) wrote the editorial marks for the textual divisions in Y.

2) The Winchester scribes wrote guide letters in W by following the editorial marks in Y.

3) Red initial letters were written in W according to the guide letters.

4) Caxton rewrote the Roman War episode, possibly consulting the *Chronicles of England.*

5) Caxton consulted the textual divisions in W and divided his 'copye', the archetype X into books and chapters.

6) The compositors, following the editorial marks written by Caxton in his 'copye', the archetype, type-set the text with book and chapter divisions.

I assume that X, the lost archetype, and Y are copies without textual divisions; Y is a lost intermediate copy, and R is a lost copy of the Roman War episode newly written by Caxton.

CONCLUSION

Today, the situation in Malory studies is very different from what it was when Vinaver's first edition was published. The present study discusses physical evidence which Vinaver did not take into account, and reveals a complicated relationship between the Winchester manuscript and Caxton's edition. Needless to say, the new physical evidence does not diminish the value of Vinaver's edition. As Hellinga mentions in the conclusion of her essay, 'for a text of this size, the variants can of course never be discussed exhaustively in spite of Professor Vinaver's great edition'.[1] Nevertheless, it is now essential to reconsider Vinaver's edition. A 'nearly diplomatic' critical edition of the Winchester manuscript is no longer an option.

The new stemma, which has been proposed in this study, suggests the importance of reconstructing Caxton's setting-copy. If Caxton set his text from the archetype, the readings of his setting-copy must be closer to Malory's original intentions than those of Winchester, despite the fact that Winchester may have influenced the Caxton in some respects, and particularly with regard to the textual divisions. Caxton's book is the product of two kinds of alterations by two parties, that is, deliberate alterations and unconscious errors, by Caxton and his compositors. It has been suggested that the Winchester scribes also changed the text both consciously and unconsciously. An editor of Malory can no longer be allowed to purge the scribal errors in the manuscript by some mechanical process, no matter how refined, and otherwise preserve the Winchester readings as they stand. He now has an obligation to edit the *Morte Darthur* more radically, using not only the existing texts and Malory's sources, but also taking full account of the habits of Caxton and his compositors. A judicious investigation into Malory and Caxton from this perspective would help to recreate the most authentic version of what Sir Thomas Malory finally intended.

---

[1] Lotte Hellinga, 'The Malory Manuscript and Caxton', in *Aspects of Malory*, ed. by Toshiyuki Takamiya and Derek Brewer, Arthurian Studies, 1 (Cambridge: Brewer, 1981), pp. 127–41 and 220–21 (p. 137).

1. Caxton's Pages with Six or More Paraphs

q2v

And thenne he callyd vnto hym syr Marhaus the good knyght that was nobly preued/and a knyghte of the table ro-
unde/And this Marhaus was broder vnto the quene of Ir-
land/ ¶ Thenne the kynge sayd thus/ Fayr broder sir Mar-
5 haus I praye yow goo in to Cornewaile for my sake and do
bataille for our truage that of ryght we oughte to haue/and
what someuer ye spende ye shalle haue suffycyently more than
ye shal nede/Syre saide Marhaus wete ye wel that I shalle
not be lothe to doo bataille in the ryght of you and your land
10 with the best knyght of the table rounde / for I knowe them
for the moost party what ben theire dedes/ and for to auaunce
my dedes and to encreace my worship I wylle ryght gladly
goo vnto this iourneye for oure ryghte
¶ Soo in alle haste there was made purueaunce for syr mar-
15 haus/and he hadde al thynge that to hym nedes/and soo he departed out of Irland / and arryued vp in Cornewaile euen
fast by the castel of Tyntagil/ And whan kynge Marke vnderstood that he was there arryued to fyghte for Irland /
¶ Thenne made kynge marke grete sorou whan he vnderstood
20 that the good and noble knyghte sir Marhaus was come /
For they knewe no knyght that durste haue adoo with hym/
For at that tyme syr Marhaus was called one of the famo-
sest and renoumed knyghtes of the world
¶ And thus syre Marhaus abode in the see/ and euery daye
25 he sente vnto kynge Marke for to paye the truage that was
behynde of seuen yere / outher els to fynde a knyght to fyghte
with hym for the truage / This maner of message syr Marhaus sente dayly vnto kynge Marke/ ¶ Thenne they of
Cornewayle lete make cryes in euery place that what knyght
30 wold fyghte for to saue the truage of Cornewaile he sholde
be rewarded soo that he sholde fare the better the terme of hys
lyf/ ¶ Thenne some of the Barons sayde to kynge
Marke / and counceiled hym to sende to the courte of kynge
Arthur for to seke syr Launcelot du lake that was that ty-
35 me named for the merueilloust knyght of alle the worlde /
¶ Thenne there were somme other Barons that counceylled
the kynge not to doo soo & said that it was labour in vayn/

q3v

regardꝫ vnto her/Also she sente hym a lytyl bracelet that was
passynge fayre/ ¶But whan the kynges doughter vnderstood
that syre Trystram wold not loue her/as the book sayth/she
dyed for sorou/ ¶ And thenne the same squyer that broughte
the letter and the bracelet came agayne vnto syr Trystram/as
after ye shalle here in the tale   ¶ Soo this yonge
syr Trystram rode vnto his eme kynge Marke of Cornewa-
yle/¶ And whanne he came there/he herd say that ther wold
no knyghte fyghte with syre Marhaus/Thenne sayd sir Tristram vnto his eme and sayd/syre yf ye wylle gyue me thor-
dre of knyghthode/I wille do bataille with syr Marhaus/
What are ye sayd the kynge and from whens be ye comen/Sir
sayd Trystram I come fro kynge Melyodas that wedded your syster and a gentylman wete ye wel I am
¶ Kynge Marke beheld sir Trystram and sawe that he was
but a yonge man of age / But he was passyngly wel maade
and bygge/¶ Faire syr sayd the kynge what is your name
and where were ye borne/Syr sayd he agayne / my name is
Trystram/and in the countreye of Lyones was I borne /
Ye saye wel sayd the kynge/ and yf ye wille do this batayll
I shalle make yow knyghte / Therfore I come to you sayd
syre Trystram and for none other cause
¶ But thenne kynge Marke made hym knyghte/And there
with al anone as he had made hym knyght he sente a messa-
ger vnto syre Marhaus with letters that sayd / that he hadde
fonde a yonge knyghte redy for to take the bataile to the vtter
mest/Hit may wel be sayd syre Marhaus/¶ But telle kynge
Marke I wille not fyghte with no knyghte but he be of blo-
ood royal/that is to saye outher kynges sone outher quenes.
sone borne of a prynce or pryncesse/
¶ Whanne kynge Marke vnderstood that / he sente for syre
Trystram de Lyones and wolde hym what was the answer of
syr Marhaus/¶ Thenne sayd syre Trystram sythen that he se
yth soo/lete hym wete that I am comen of fader syde and mo
der syde of as noble blood as he is/¶ For syr now shalle ye
knowe that I am kynge Melyodas sone borne of your own
syster dame Elyzabeth that dyed in the forest in the byrthe of
me/O Jhesu sayd kynge Mark ye are welcome faire nevewe

I sent hit hym for to assay his lady/ ¶And yf she be true to
hym she shal preue her/ Soo the knyghte wente his waye vnto
kynge Marke and broughte hym that ryche horne / and sayd
that sir Lamorak sente hit hym / and there to he told hym the
5 vertue of that horne   ¶Thenne the kynge maade
Quene Isoud to drynke therof/ and an honderd ladyes/ and
there were but four ladyes of alle tho that dranke clene/
¶Allas saide kynge Marke this is a grete despyte/ and swa
re a grete othe/ that she shold be brente and the other ladyes /
10 ¶Thenne the Barons gadred them to gyder and said playn
ly they wold not haue tho ladyes brente for an horne maade
by sorcery that came from as fals a sorceresse and wytche as tho
was lyuynge/ For that horne dyd neuer good but caused stryf
and debate/ and allweyes in her dayes she had ben an enemy to
15 alle true louers/ Soo there were many knyghtes made their a-
uowe/ and euer they met with Morgan le fay that they wold
shewe her short curtosye/ ¶Also sir Tristram was passynge
wrothe that sire Lamorak sente that horne vnto kynge Marke
for wel he knewe that hit was done in the despyte of hym /
20 And therfor he thoughte to quyte sire Lamorak/ ¶Thenne
syre Tristram vsed dayly and nyghtely to go to quene Isoud
whanne he myght/ and euer syre Andred his cosyn watched
hym nyght and daye for to take hym with la Beale Isoud/
And soo vpon a nyght syre Andred aspyed the houre and the
25 tyme whan sir Tristram wente to his lady/ ¶Thenne syre
Andred gate vnto hym twelue knyghtes/ and at mydnyghte
he sette vpon sire Tristram secretely and sodenly/ and there sire
Tristram was take naked a bedde with la Beale Isoud / and
thenne was he boūd hande and foot/ and soo was he kepte vn
30 tyl daye/ ¶And thenne by the assent of kynge Marke and of
syre Andred and of somme of the Barons syre Tristram was
ledde vnto a chappel that stode vpon the see rockes there for to
take his Iugement/ and soo he was ledde bounden with fourty
knyghtes/ And whan sire Tristram sawe that there was none
35 other boote/ But nedes that he must dye/ thenne said he fayr lor-
des remembre what I haue done for the Countreye of Cornewaile / and in what Ieopardy I haue ben in for the wele of
you alle/ For whan I fouzt for the truage of cornewaile with

haue dyed/ Nay nay saide sire Tristram/ Dynadan/ neuer drede
the/ for I am here hole/ & of this wounde I shal soone be hole
by the mercy of god/ ⸿ By that sir Dynadan was ware
where came palomydes rydynge streyght vpon them / And
thenne syre Tristram was ware that syre Palomydes came to
haue destroyed hym /and so syre Dynadan gaf hym warnyng
and saide sir Tristram my lord ye are soo sore wounded that
ye may not haue adoo with hym / therfore I wille ryde agey-
nst hym and doo to hym what I maye/ And yf I be slayne
ye maye praye for my soule and in the meane whyle ye maye
withdrawe you and goo in to the castel/ or in the foreste that
he shalle not mete with you/ ⸿ Syre Tristram
smyled and said I thanke you syre Dynadan of your good
wylle/ But ye shalle wete that I am able to handle hym/ And
thenne anone hastely he armed hym and toke his hors/and a
grete spere in his hand and said to syre Dynadan Adieu / &
rode toward syre Palamydes a softe paas
⸿ Thenne whanne sire Palomydes sawe that/ he made counte-
naunce to amende his hors / but he dyd hit for this cause/ For
he abode sire Gaherys that came after hym/⸿ And whanne he
was come he rode toward syre Tristram / ⸿ Thenne syre Tristram sente vnto syr palomydes and requyred hym to juste with
hym/ And yf he smote doune sir Palomydes/ he wold doo no
more to hym/ And yf it so happend that sire Palomydes smo
te doune syr Tristram he badde hym do his vtteraunce/ So they
were accorded/ thenne they mette to gyders/ and syre Tristram
smote doune sir palomydes / that he had a greuous falle / soo
that he laye stylle as he hadde ben dede/ And thenne sire Trystram ranne vpon syr Gaherys/ and he wold not haue justed
But whether he wolde or not syre Tristram smote hym ouer
his hors croupe that he laye stylle as though he had ben dede /
And thenne syr Tristram rode his waye and lefte syre Phersy-
des squyer within the pauelions / and syre Tristram and syre
Dynadan rode to an old knyghtes place to lodge them/ And
that olde knyght had fyue sones at the turnement/ for whome
he prayed god hertely for their comyng home/ ⸿ And so as the
frensshe booke saith they cam home al/v/ wel beten / And whan
syr Tristram departed in to the forest syr Launcelot held allwey

B3r

tlvo knyghtes/for they fought more than tlvo houres / And
there they bothe bledde soo moche bloode/that alle may merueyl
led/that euer they myght endure hit/
¶ And so at the laste by bothe their assentes they were made
frendes and sworne bretheren for euer/ and no man can Juge
the better knyght/ And now is sir Tristram made a knyghte
of the rounde table/and he sytteth in the sege of the noble knyght sire Marhaus/   ¶ By my hede said sir
Palomydes syre Tristram is ferre bygger than sir Launcelot/
and the hardyer knyght/   ¶ Haue ye assayed them
bothe saide syre Dynadan/¶ I haue sene syre Tristram fyghte said syre Palomydes /But neuer sire Launcelot/to my we-
tynge/But at the fontayne where sire Launcelot lay on slepe
there with one spere he smote doune sire Tristram/and me said
Palomydes/But at that tyme they knewe not eyther other
Faire knyghte said sir Dynadan as for sir Launcelot and sir
Tristram lete them be/for the werst of them wille not be lyght-
ly matched of no knyghtes that I knowe lyuynge/
No said sire Palomydes good defende But and I had a quar-
rel to the better of them bothe/ I wolde with as good a wylle
fyghte with hym as with yow
¶ Syre I requyre you telle me your name and in good feith
I shalle holde you company/tyl that we come to Camelot/and
there shall ye haue grete worship now at this grete turnement
for there shalle be the Quene Gueneuer/ and la Beale Isoud
of Cornewaile / wete yow wel syre knyght for the loue of la
Beale Isoud I wille be there and els not/ But I wille not ha
ue adoo in kynge Arthurs courte/Sir said Dynadan I shal
ryde with yow and doo you seruyse/so ye wille telle me youre
name/Syre ye shalle vnderstonde my name is syre Palomydes
brother to Safere the good and noble knyghte / And syre
Segwarydes and I be the Sarasyns borne of fader and mo-
der/   ¶ Syre said sire Dynadan I thanke you
moche/for the tellyng of your name/For I am gladde of that
I knowe your name/& I promyse you by the feyth of my body
ye shalle not be hurte by me by my wille/But rather be auaun-
ced/And therto wille I helpe yow with all my power I promyse you/doubte ye not / And certaynly on my lyf ye shalle
                                                    B iij

D2r

and ypon the hyghe ordre of knyghthode that sholb be reuengyd
ypon kynge Marke for the dethe of thy fader / andz there with
all she swouned/ Thenne Alysander lepte to his moder / andz
toke her vp in his armes andz sayd Fair moder ye haue gyuen
5 me a grete charge/andz here I promyse yolb I shalle be auen
gyd ypon kynge Marke / whanne that I may /andz that I
promyse to godz andz to yolb ¶ Soo this feest was
endydz/andz the conestabyl by the aduyse of anglydes lete pur
ueye that Alysander was wel horsedz and harneysid/Thenne
10 he justedz with his twenty felalbes that were made knyghtes
with hym/but for to make a shorte tale he ouerthrewe alle tho
twenty that none myght withstande hym a buffet/¶ Thenne
one of tho knyghtes departedz vnto kynge Marke/andz told
hym alle holb Alysander was maade knyght / andz alle the
15 charge that his moder gaf hym as ye haue herdz afore tyme
¶ Allas fals treason saidz kynge Marke I wende that yonge traitour hadz ben dede/Allas whome may I truste/Andz
there with alle kynge Marke toke a sberdz in his handz/andz
soughte sire Sadok from chamber to chamber to slee hym/
20 ¶ Whanne sir Sadok salbe kynge Marke come with his suerd
in his handz/he saydz thus/Belbare kynge Marke andz come
not nyghe me/for wete thou wel that I sauedz Alysander his
lyf/of whiche I neuer repente me / for thou falsly andz co-
wardly slelbe his fader Boudlyn trayturly for his goodz
25 ddes/wherfore I pray almyghty Jhesu sende Alysander myg-
ghte andz strengthe to be reuengyd ypon the/andz nolb belbare
kynge Marke of yonge Alysander/for he is made a knyght/
¶ Alas saidz kynge Marke that euer I sholdz bere a traytour saye soo afore me/¶ Andz there with foure knyghtes of
30 kynge Markes drewe theire sberdes to slee syr Sadok / but
anone sir Sadok slelbe hem alle in kynge Markes presence /
Andz thenne sir Sadok past forthe in to his chamber/andz toke his hors andz his harneis / andz rode on his waye a goodz
paas/For there was neyther syr Tristram / neyther syr Dy-
35 nas nor syr Fergus that wold sir Sadok ony euylle wylle/
¶ Thenne was kynge Marke wrothe/and thoughte to destro-
ye syr Alysander andz syre Sadok that hadz sauedz hym / for
kynge Marke dredde andz hated Alisander moost of ony man

D ij

E1v

Chalcyns of Clarence and in his gouernaunce there came
a knyghte that hyghte Elys la noyre/ And there encountred
with hym kynge Bagdemagus / and he smote Elys that he
made hym to auoyde his sadel/ ¶ Soo the Duke Chalcyns of
5 Clarence dyd there grete dedes of armes/and of soo late as
he came in the thyrdde daye there was no man dyd soo wel ex-
cepte kynge Bagdemagus and sire Palomydes that the pryce
Was gyuen that day to kynge Bagdemagus /
¶ And thenne they rydwe vnto lodgynge and vnarmed hem
10 and wente to the feest/ ¶ Ryght soo came Dynadan and moc-
ked and japed with kynge Bagdemagus that alle knyghtes laugh at hym/for he was a fyne japer and loued
alle good knyghtes/ ¶ Soo anone as they had
dyned/ there came a Varlet beryng foure speres on his back/ &
15 he came to Palomydes/ & sayd thus / here is a knyghte by sith
sent yow the choyse of foure speres/and requyreth yow for your lady sake to take that one half of these speres / and Juste
With hym in the felde/ ¶ Telle hym said Palomydes I wyll
not fayle hym / whanne sire Galahalt wyste of this/he badde
20 Palomydes make hym redy/ ¶ So the Quene Gueneuer the
haute prynce and sire Launcelot they were set vpon scaffoldes to gyue the Jugement of these two knyghtes /
¶ Thenne sire Palomydes and the straunge knyght ranne so
egerly to gyders that their speres braste to their handes/ Anon
25 with alle eyther of them toke a grete spere in his hand/ and
alle to sheuered them in pyeces / And thenne eyther toke a
gretter spere/ And thenne the knyghte smote doune syre Palomydes hors and man to the erthe / And as he wolde haue
passed ouer hym/the straunge knyghtes hors stumbled and
30 felle doune vpon Palomydes ¶ Thenne they
drewe their swerdes and lasshed to gyders wonderly sore a grete whyle/ ¶ Thenne the haute prynce and sire Launcelot sayd
they sawe neuer two knyghtes fyghte better than they dyd /
But euer the straunge knyght doubled his strokes/ and putte
35 Palomydes abak/ thow with alle the haute prynce cryed hoo /
and thenne they wente to lodgynge/ And whanne they were
vnarmed/they knewe hit was the noble knyzt syr Lamorak
¶ Whanne syr Launcelot knewe that hit was sir Lamorak he

E4r

Gueneuer/Thenne sir Launcelot dyd as he was requyred /
Thenne sire Lamorak andr he smote doune many knyghtes/ &
racydr of helmes/andr drofe alle the knyghtes afore them
Andr soo sire Launxelot smote doune sire Dynadan/andr ma=
5 de his men to vnarme hym/ andr soo brought hym to the quene
andr the haute prynx andr they lough at dynadan so sore that
they myghte not stande/ wel saidr sire Dynadan yet haue I no
shame/for the oldr shrewe sire Launcelot smote me doune/ So
they wente to dyuer/alle the Courte andr goodr sporte at Dy=
10 nadan   ¶ Thenne whanne the dyner was done/they
blewe to the felde to beholde sire Palomydes andr Corsabryn /
Syre Palomydes pyght his penfell in myddes of the felde / &
thene they hurtled to gydere with their speres as it were thon
der/andr eyther smote other to the erthe/Andr thenne they pul
15 ledr oute their swerdes/andr dressidr their sheldes/andr lasshed
to gydere myghtely as myghty knyztes/that wel nyghe there
was no pyece of harneis woldr holdr them/for this Corsabryn
was a passynge felonous knyghte / Corsabryn saidr Palomy=
des wylte thow releace me yondr damoysel/andr the penfell /
20 Thenne was Corsabryn wrothe oute of mesure/ andr gaf Palo
mydes suche a buffet that he kneledr on his knee/
¶ Thenne Palomydes arose lyghtely / andr smote hym vpon
the helme/that he felle doune ryzt to the erthe/ Andr ther with
he racydr of his helme/ andr saydr Corsabryn yelde the or ellys
25 thou shalt dye of my handes / Fy on the saidr Corsabryn/ doo
thy werst/thenne he smote of his hede/Andr ther with all cam
a stynke of his body whan the soule departedr/ that ther myzt
no body abyde the sauoure/Soo was the corps hidde alwey
andr buryedr in a woodr by cause he was a paynym/
30 ¶ Thenne they blewe vnto lodgynge / andr Palomydes was
vnarmedr   ¶ Thenne he wente vnto Quene Gue=
neuer/to the haute prynx/andr to syre Launcelot/¶ Syre sayd
the haute prynce/ here haue ye sene this day a grete myrakel by
Corsabryn/what sauour ther was whanne the soule departedr
35 from the body/There for syre we wylle requyre yow to take the
baptym vpon yow/andr I promyse yow alle knyghtes wyll
sette the more by yow/andr say more worshhip by yow
¶ Syre saidr Palomydes I wille that ye alle knowe / that in
E iiij

F2r

Fair knyghtes said sir Palomydes I canne telle yow tydyn-
ges/ What is that said tho knyghtes / Syrs wete ye wel that
kynge Marke is put in pryson by his owne knyghtes / and
alle was for loue of sire Tristram/ for kynge Marke hadde put
5 sire Tristram thryes in pryson / And ones sire Percyuale delyuerd the noble knyghte sire Tristram oute of pryson
¶And at the laste tyme Quene La beale Isoud delyuerd
hym / and wente clerely alweye with hym in to this rame/ &
alle this whyle kynge Marke the fals traytour is in pryson /
10 Is this trouthe said Palomydes/ Thenne shall we hastely be ≁
re of sire Tristram/ And as for to say that I loue la Beale
Isoud peramoure I dare make good that I doo / and that
she hath my seruyse aboue alle other ladyes / and shalle haue
the terme of my lyf/ And ryght so as they stood talkynge /
15 they salhe afore them where came a knyghte alle armed on a
grete hors/ and one of his men bare his sheld / and the other
his spere/ And anone as that knyght aspyed them he gate
his sheld and his spere/and dressid hym to Juste
¶Fair felawes said sire Palomydes yonder is a knyghte wil
20 Juste with vs/lete see whiche of vs shalle encountre with hym
for I see wel he is of the courte of kynge Arthur
¶It shalle not be longe or ye be mette with alle said sire Palomydes / for I fonde neuer noo knyght in my queste of this
Glastynge beest/But and ye wold Juste I neuer refused hym
25 ¶As wel may I said Breuse saunz pyte folowe that beest
as ye/Thenne shalle ye doo bataille with me said Palomydes/
Soo sire Palomydes dressid hym vnto that other knyghte
sire Bleoberys that was a ful noble knyghte nyghe kynne
vnto sire Launcelot / And soo they mette soo harde / that syre
30 Palomydes felle to the erthe hors and alle/
Thenne sir Bleoberis cryed a lowde and said thus/make the
redy thou fals traytour knyghte Breuse saunz pyte/for wete
thow certaynly I wille haue adoo with the to the vtteraunce
for the noble knyghtes and ladyes that thou hast falsly bi-
35 trayed ¶Whanne this false knyght and traitour
Breuse saunz pyte herde hym saye soo/ he took his hors by the
brydel and fledde his waye/as fast as euer his hors myghte
renne/for sore he was of hym aferd/¶Whan sir Bleoberys

R3r

of the rotten tree and of the whyte floures / syre I shalle telle
yow a parte now and the other dele to morowe / The whyte fo-
ule betokeneth a gentyl woman fayr and ryche whiche loued
the peramours / and fals loued the longe
5 ¶ And yf thou warne her loue she shalle goo dye anone yf
thou haue no pyte on her / that sygnefyeth the gret byrd / the
whiche shalle make the to warne her / ¶ Now for noo fere that
thou hast ne for no drede that thou haste of god / thou shalt
not warne her but thou woldest not do hit for to be holden chast
10 for to conquere the loos of the veyne glory of the world / for
that shalle befalle the now and thou warne her that Laimer ꝫ
bot the good knyght thy cosyn shalle dye / And therfore men
shalle now saye f thou art a man sleer / both of thy broder syre
Lyonel and of thy cosyn syre Launcelot du Lake / the whiche
15 thou myghtest haue saued and resolued easyly / But thou
wenest to resolue a mayde whiche pertyneth no thynge to the
¶ Now loke thou whether hit had ben gretter harme of thy
broders deth or els to haue suffred her to haue lost her mayden-
hode / ¶ Thenne asked he hym haste
20 thou herd the tokens of thy dreme the whiche I haue told to
yow / Ye forsothe sayd syre Bors / alle youre exposycyon and
declarynge of my dreme I haue wel understande and herd /
Thenne said the man in this Black clothynge / whenne is hit in
thy defaute yf syre Launcelot thy cosyn dye / ¶ Syre said bors
25 that were me lothe / for wete ye wel there is no thynge in the
world But I had leuer doo hit than to see my lord syre Laun
celot du Lake to dye in my defaute
Chese ye now the one or the other said the good man / And
thenne he led syre Bors in to an hyghe toure / and there he
30 fonde knyghtes and ladyes tho ladyes sayde he was wel
come / and soo they unarmed hym / ¶ And whanne he was in
his dobblet / men broughte hym a mantel furred with ermyn
and putte hit aboute hym / and thenne they made hym suche che
re that he hadde forgeten alle his sorowe and anguysshe /
35 and only sette his herte in these delytes and deyntees / e tooke
noo thoughte more for his broder syre Lyonel nepther of syre
Launcelot du Lake his cosyn / And anone came oute of a chamber to hym the fayrest lady that euer he sawe e more rycher

2. Variants in Caxton's Pages with Six or More Paraphs

The first significant discoveries about Caxton's setting-copy were made by Lotte Hellinga, who focused on the variants observed in Caxton's page divisions. She found that some words are repeated at the end of sig. g1v and at the beginning of sig. g2r. From this, she concludes that the casting-off marks found in this place made it 'difficult for the compositor to decide which line was indicated'.[1] In other words, the compositor who type-set g1v believed that marked line in the setting-copy should be the last line of the page, whereas the compositor of g2r believed that the line indicated the first line of the page. On this basis, Hellinga successfully worked out three lines of Caxton's setting-copy. A similar procedure has been followed by Toshiyuki Takamiya.[2]

In this Appendix, Caxton's pages with six or more paraphs will be examined. The readings of Caxton's setting-copy which correspond to these pages would have caused serious problems in the casting-off process.

Most of the words added to the pages with six or more paraphs appear in Vinaver's critical apparatus simply as variants. However, Vinaver regards some of these additional words as being probably closer to Malory's intention than the Winchester text. Asterisks (*) by these words show that Vinaver considers that Caxton's reading is 'preferable' to that of the base text, or that Caxton's reading is likely to throw some light upon that of Winchester. Moreover, even without the support of French sources, Vinaver borrows two of these phrases to emend the Winchester text.[3] Since he made no specific comments regarding these emendations, it is difficult to determine what criteria Vinaver used for these decisions.

It can be said of all the words added in <type B-6+> pages that they do not obstruct the flow of the sentences, nor do they change the meaning of what is being said. It seems to be highly feasible to interpret these words as being compositors' padding, which was carefully designed so as not to alter the meaning of the sentence. Doublets were often used to lengthen the text.[4]

---

[1] Lotte Hellinga, *Caxton in Focus: The Beginning of Printing in England* (London: British Library, 1982), p. 93.

[2] See pp. 42–43 above.

[3] Vinaver distinguished the emendations from the body of the text by using [ ] for the readings borrowed from the Caxton without the support of *F*, Malory's French sources as represented by the extant manuscripts. See *The Works of Sir Thomas Malory*, ed. by Eugène Vinaver, 3rd edn, rev. by P. J. C. Field, 3 vols (Oxford: Clarendon Press, 1990), pp. cxxii–cxxiii.

[4] See pp. 38–41 above.

Although the Winchester manuscript is necessarily our basis for comparison, one must always remember that the Winchester text and the Caxton are in a collateral relationship. In some of the cases where the Caxton has a fuller reading than Winchester, this will be because Winchester has lost words in transmission from the archetype X rather than because the Caxton has gained them, by compositors' padding or in any other way. Caxton's readings, which are supported by Malory's sources, or whose counterparts in Winchester do not make sense, may well be authorial. However, the following examples are clear evidence of compositors' padding, because they are supported by other proofs besides the copy-fitting problems.

In sig. q2v, line 31, for example, a compositor replaced 'to' in Winchester with the phrase 'soo that he sholde':

> sig. q2v, 377/1–8[5]
> 24   ¶And thus syre Marhaus abode in the see / and euery daye
> 25   he sente vnto kynge Marke for to paye the truage that was
> 26   behynde *of* seuen yere / outher els to fynde a knyght to fyghte
> 27   with hym for the truage / This maner of message syre Mar-
> 28   haus sente *dayly* vnto kynge Marke / -------- ¶Thenne they of
> 29   Cornewayle lete make cryes *in euery place* that what knyght
> 30   wold fyghte for to saue the truage of Cornewaile he sholde
> 31   be rewarded *soo that he sholde* fare the better *the* terme of hys
> 32   lyf /--------------¶

This rephrasing, along with Hellinga's study, strongly supports the theory that a compositor freely changed the words in order to adjust the length of the text. Hellinga particularly focused on the end of sig. g1v, 'entente *that I shold* slee kynge Arthur her broder / For ye shall vnderstand', and the beginning of the next page, sig. g2r, which reads: 'entente *to* slee kyng Arthur her broder / for ye shal vnderstand.' The compositor who set g2r thought that the page would start with the line beginning with 'entente'. The compositor who set g1v, on the other hand, 'thought that the stroke in his exemplar indicated the line *following* the one beginning with *entente* as the spot

---

[5] All citations from the *Morte* in this Appendix are taken from *Sir Thomas Malory, 'Le Morte D'Arthur', Printed by William Caxton 1485: Facsimile*, intro. by Paul Needham (London: Scolar Press, 1976), otherwise noted; the variants found only in the Caxton are indicated by italicised bold letters. The white spaces in the Caxton are presented by '------'. Caxton's signature numbers are followed by Vinaver's page and line numbers. Vinaver's interpretations are shown using his own marks for emendations, that is, * and [ ]. All the <type B-6+> pages are reproduced in Appendix 1 with the line numbers; the additions are marked with rectangles.

where g 2 recto had started – wishful thinking, no doubt, as he had obviously too much space on his hands'.[6] Thus, Hellinga considers that the compositor replaced 'to' with 'that I shold'. As this alteration of 'to' into 'that [subject] shold' is similar to the one seen in q2v, 'to' into 'soo that he sholde', the alteration in q2v can be interpreted as a compositor's device.

Another example of a compositor's padding can be found in sig. z4r:

sig. z4r, 533/7–12
26   and syre Tristram
27 smote doune sir palomydes / that he had a greuous falle / ***soo***
28 ***that he*** laye stylle as he hadde ben dede / And thenne sire Trys-
29 tram ranne vpon syr Gaherys / and he wold not haue justed
30 But whether he wolde or not syre Tristram smote hym ouer
31 his hors croupe that he laye stylle *__as though he had ben dede__* /

The phrase in line 31 is seemingly important because it explains the situation more vividly. Vinaver places an asterisk by the Caxton reading. However, three lines above, both Winchester and the Caxton depict Sir Palomydes lying still 'as he hadde ben dede', a passage which should also be found in the setting-copy of Caxton. The repetition of the same passage within only three lines is unlikely to be 'a feature of Malory's straightforward prose'.[7] This seems to have happened because the need to lengthen the text led the compositor to imitate the expression just above.

In the pages with six or more paraphs, there are other examples where a compositor has repeated the earlier sentences:

sig. E4r, 666/ 23–24
36   ***I promyse yow*** alle knyghtes wyll
37 sette the more by yow / *__and say more worship by yow__*---------

Although the expression slightly differs in its meaning, 'say more worship by yow' is nothing but a repetition of 'sette the more by yow'. Both of them signify that 'people bestow honour on him'. 'I promyse yow' is also just a repetition of a vow.

It is also interesting that the same phrase 'I promyse yow' is inserted twice at the end of another <type B-6+> page, sig. B3r. Most of the words in the last five lines of this page do not appear in the Winchester manuscript:

---

[6] Hellinga, *Caxton in Focus*, p. 94.

[7] Terence McCarthy, 'Caxton and the Text of Malory's Book 2', *Modern Philology*, 71 (1973), 144–52 (p. 149).

sig. B3r, 597/1–3
```
33                        ----------------¶Syre said sire Dynadan I thanke you
34    *moche / for the tellyng of your name / For I am gladde of that
35    I knowe your name / & *I promyse you by the feyth of my body
36    ye shalle not be hurte by me *by my will / but rather be auaun-
37    ced / And *therto wille I helpe yow with all my power I pro-
38    myse you / *doubte ye not / And certaynly on my lyf ye shalle
```

Despite its numerous variants, all the additional words observed at the bottom of this page are either repetition, emphasis, or words expressing a vow. 'Moche' simply emphasises his thanks; 'for the tellyng of your name' is a paraphrase of 'I am gladde of that I knowe your name'; and the rest of them are all words of vows. It is important to realise that 'and certaynly' in the last line is clearly Caxtonian since none of the words derived from 'certain' appears in the Winchester manuscript.[8] Furthermore, the same word 'certaynly' is inserted in another <type B-6+> page, sig. F2r, line 33 only in the Caxton version.[9]

Most of the phrases, which appear only in Caxton's R3r, do not contribute to the meaning of the text either:

sig. R3r, 964/6–11
```
17    ¶Now loke thow whether hit had ben gretter harme of thy
18    broders deth or els to haue suffred her to haue lost her mayden-
19    hode /-----------------------------------¶Thenne asked he hym haste
20    thow herd the tokens of thy dreme *the whiche I haue told to
21    yow / Ye *forsothe sayd syre Bors / *alle youre exposycyon and
22    declarynge of my dreme I haue wel vnderstande and herd /
23    Thenne said the man in this black clothynge / thenne is hit in
```

It is clear from the context that the man has already interpreted Sir Bors's dream, and thus, 'the whiche I haue told to yow' is rather unnecessary. 'Alle youre exposycyon and declarynge of my dreme I haue wel vnderstande and herd' could be explained just by answering 'Yes'. The entire doublet, both 'exposycyon and declarynge', is added in this case. Interestingly enough, the words 'exposycyon' and 'declarynge', or their derivatives do not appear at all in Malory's prose. In Caxton's prose, on the other hand, 'exposycyon' is not

---

[8] See *A Concordance to 'The Works of Sir Thomas Malory'*, ed. by Tomomi Kato (Tokyo: University of Tokyo Press, 1974), and *A Concordance to Caxton's Own Prose,* ed. by Kiyokazu Mizobata (Tokyo: Shohakusha, 1990).

[9] See p. 40 above.

used, but 'declare' appears as often as eleven times.[10] The description of the man 'in this black clothynge' seems to be taken from similar expressions in previous lines, 'a man clothed in a religious wede, and rode on a stronge blacke horse, blacker than a byry' (962/28–29).

Besides, in sig. R3r, many additions which do not affect the meaning at all are spread throughout this page: 'she shalle *goo* dye anone' (line 5); 'And therfore men shalle *now* saye' (line 13); 'launcelot *du lake*' (lines 14 and 27); 'thow myghtest haue *saued and* rescowed easyly' (line 15); 'Syre said bors that were me lothe / for *wete ye wel* ' (line 25); '*said the good man / And* thenne he led' (line 28).

Taking into account this situation, the following passage needs reinterpretation:

> sig. R3r, 964/19–25
> 31 ¶And whanne he was in
> 32 his dobblet / men broughte hym a mantel furred with ermyn
> 33 and putte hit aboute hym / and thenne they made hym suche che
> 34 re that he hadde forgeten *alle* his sorowe [*and anguysshe /*
> 35 *and only sette his herte in these delytes and deyntees / & tooke*
> 36 *noo thoughte more for his broder syre Lyonel neyther of syre*
> 37 *Launcelot du lake his cosyn*] / And anone came oute of

Vinaver has taken this long reading from the Caxton 'on the assumption that their loss was caused by an "eyeskip" from *and anguysshe* to *and anone*'.[11]

However, the language in this passage is peculiarly un-Malorian. The words 'anguysshe', 'delytes' and 'deyntees' appear only few times (two, three and six times respectively, apart from R3r) in the whole of the story.[12] In sig. R3r, Sir Bors is blamed by a priest: 'thow art a man sleer / both of thy **broder syre Lyonel** and of thy **cosyn syre launcelot du lake**' (lines 13–14). This sentence is repeated in lines 36–37 stating that Sir Bors did not think of 'his **broder syre Lyonel** neyther of **syre Launcelot du lake his cosyn**'. In the next page, Sir Bors, unable to forget about Lyonel and Lancelot, rejects the fair lady's temptation: 'there ys no lady in thys worlde whos wylle I wolde fullfylle as of thys thynge. She ought nat desire hit, for my brothir lyeth dede, which was slayne ryght late'.[13] Vinaver's theory that the Winchester

---

[10] The following variants are seen: 'declaracion' (2 times), 'declare' (2), 'declared' (3), 'declareth' (2) and 'declaryng' (2).

[11] *Works*, p. 1566.

[12] The variants are 'anguysshe', (967/7 and 972/7); 'delytes' (333/12, 1046/30 and 1121/1) and 'deyntees' (187/8, 187/12, 224/28, 318/13, 956/23 and 1048/29).

[13] *Works*, p. 965.

manuscript's scribe carried out an eye-skip is not impossible. However, it is more natural to consider that the variants were the result of the text-lengthening by Caxton's compositor, who read only this page and did not realise that Sir Bors would immediately leave the situation, thinking of Lyonel and Launcelot.

These researches on Caxton's readings are based on a comparison made with Winchester, which was clearly not Caxton's setting-copy. As was said at the beginning of this Appendix, it needs to be kept in mind that some of Caxton's variants may be authorial. However, when reconstructing Malory's readings, it is important also to bear in mind that many of the variants observed in the pages with six or more paraphs hardly contribute to the content of the lines. In order to create future critical editions, every kind of evidence will need to be examined. In the examples discussed in this Appendix, evidence derived from the printing techniques has been used as a kind of demonstration of the possibilities offered by one type of evidence. This evidence, I would argue, shows that Vinaver's decision to put asterisks and even square brackets against some of Caxton's readings should be reconsidered. Instead, it is often reasonable to conclude that these words were inserted by Caxton or his compositors in order to lengthen the text and make it flow seamlessly to the next page.

BIBLIOGRAPHY

1. Primary Sources

Manuscripts

London, British Library, Additional MS 59678
Vatican, Vatican Library, latin. 11441

Printed Books

Caxton, William, *Caxton's Own Prose*, ed. by N. F. Blake (London: Deutsch, 1973)

Eracles; Godefrey of Boloyne, trans. by William Caxton (Westminster, 1481), English Experience Series, 604 (New York: Da Capo Press; Amsterdam: Theatrum Orbis Terrarum, 1973), a facsimile

Le Fèvre, Raoul, *The Recuyell of the Historyes of Troye*, trans. by William Caxton (Bruges, 1473–74), a microfilm, *STC* 15375 (reel 1209)

——, *Th'istories of Jason*, trans. by William Caxton (Westminster, 1477), a microfilm, *STC* 15383 (reel 47)

Malory, Thomas, *The Winchester Malory: A Facsimile*, intro. by N. R. Ker, EETS SS 4 (London: Oxford University Press, 1976)

——, *'Le Morte D'Arthur', Printed by William Caxton 1485: Facsimile*, intro. by Paul Needham (London: Scolar Press, 1976)

——, *Caxton's Malory: A New Edition of Sir Thomas Malory's 'Le Morte Darthur' Based on the Pierpont Morgan Copy of William Caxton's Edition of 1485*, ed. by James Spisak and William Matthews, with a Dictionary of Names and Places by Bert Dillon, 2 vols (Berkeley, CA: University of California Press, 1983)

——, *The Works of Sir Thomas Malory*, ed. by Eugène Vinaver, 3rd edn, rev. by P. J. C. Field, 3 vols (Oxford: Clarendon Press, 1990)

Vyrgyle, *Eneydos*, trans. by William Caxton (Westminster, 1490), a microfilm, *STC* 24796 (reel 17)

2. Scholarship

Archibald, Elizabeth, 'Beginnings: *The Tale of King Arthur* and *King Arthur and the Emperor Lucius*', in *A Companion to Malory*, ed. by Elizabeth Archibald and A. S. G. Edwards, Arthurian Studies, 37 (Cambridge: Brewer, 1996), pp. 133–51

——, and A. S. G. Edwards, eds, *A Companion to Malory*, Arthurian Studies, 37 (Cambridge: Brewer, 1996)

Barker, Nicolas, 'Caxton's Typography', *Journal of the Printing Historical Society*, 11 (1976–77), 114–49

Beal, Peter, 'Sir Thomas Malory', in *Index of English Literary Manuscripts*, ed. by P. J. Croft, Theodore Hofmann, and John Horden (London: Mansell; New York: Bowker, 1980–), I, pt 2 (1980): *1450–1625*, ed. by Peter Beal, pp. 323–24

Bennett, J. A. W., 'Review of *The Works of Sir Thomas Malory*, ed. by Eugène Vinaver', *Review of English Studies*, 25 (1949), 161–67

——, ed., *Essays on Malory* (Oxford: Clarendon Press, 1963)

Benskin, Michael, and Margaret Laing, 'Translations and *Mischsprachen* in Middle English Manuscripts', in *So meny people longages and tonges: Philological Essays in Scots and Mediaeval English Presented to Angus McIntosh*, ed. by Michael Benskin and M. L. Samuels (Edinburgh: Benskin & Samuels, 1981), pp. 55–106

Blades, William, *The Biography and Typography of William Caxton: England's First Printer*, 2nd edn (London: Trübner, 1882)

Blake, N. F., *Caxton and his World* (London: Deutsch, 1969)

——, *Caxton: England's First Publisher* (London: Osprey, 1976)

——, ed., *William Caxton: A Bibliographical Guide* (NY: Garland, 1985)

——, 'Caxton Prepares his Edition of the *Morte Darthur*', in *William Caxton and English Literary Culture*, ed. by N. F. Blake (London: Hambledon, 1991), pp. 199–211

——, 'Manuscript to Print', in *William Caxton and English Literary Culture*, ed. by N. F. Blake (London: Hambledon, 1991), pp. 275–303

——, 'Caxton at Work: A Reconsideration', in *The Malory Debate: Essays on the Texts of 'Le Morte Darthur'*, ed. by Bonnie Wheeler, Robert L. Kindrick and Michael N. Salda, Arthurian Studies, 47 (Cambridge: Brewer, 2000), pp. 233–53

Bornstein, Diane, 'William Caxton's Chivalric Romances and the Burgundian Renaissance in England', *English Studies*, 57 (1976), 1–10

Boyd, Beverly, 'William Caxton (1422?–1491)', in *Editing Chaucer: The Great Tradition*, ed. by Paul G. Ruggiers (Norman, OK: Pilgrim Books, 1984), pp. 13–34

Brewer, Charlotte, *Editing 'Piers Plowman': The Evolution of the Text* (Cambridge: Cambridge University Press, 1996)

Brewer, D. S., 'the hoole book', in *Essays on Malory*, ed. by J. A. W. Bennett (Oxford: Clarendon Press, 1963), pp. 41–63

——, and Toshiyuki Takamiya, eds, *Aspects of Malory*, Arthurian Studies, 1 (Cambridge: Brewer, 1981)

Bühler, Curt F., 'Two Caxton Problems', *Library*, 4th ser. 20 (1939–40), 266–71

——, *The Fifteenth-Century Book: The Scribes, the Printers, the Decorators* (Philadelphia: University of Pennsylvania Press; London: Oxford University Press, 1960)

Chaytor, Henry John, 'The Medieval Reader and Textual Criticism', *Bulletin of the John Rylands Library*, 26 (1941–42), 49–56

Clair, Colin, *A History of European Printing* (London: Academic Press, 1976)

Clough, Andrea, 'Malory's *Morte Darthur*: The "Hoole Book"', *Medievalia et Humanistica*, n.s. 14 (1986), 139–56

Cooper, Helen, 'Review of *The Two Versions of Malory's 'Morte Darthur': Multiple Negation and the Editing of the Text*, by Ingrid Tieken-Boon van Ostade', *Medium Aevum*, 65 (1996), 321–22

——, 'M for Merlin: The Case of the Winchester Manuscript', in *Medieval Heritage: Essays in Honour of Tadahiro Ikegami*, ed. by Masahiko Kanno and others (Tokyo: Yushodo, 1997), pp. 93–107

——, 'Opening up the Malory Manuscript', in *The Malory Debate: Essays on the Texts of 'Le Morte Darthur'*, ed. by Bonnie Wheeler, Robert L. Kindrick and Michael N. Salda, Arthurian Studies, 47 (Cambridge: Brewer, 2000), pp. 255–84

De Hamel, Christopher, *Scribes and Illuminators* (London: British Museum Press, 1992)

Donaghey, Brian, 'William Thynne's Collected Edition of Chaucer: Some Bibliographical Considerations', in *Texts and their Contexts: Papers from the Early Book Society*, ed. by John Scattergood and Julia Boffey (Dublin: Four Courts Press, 1997), pp. 150–64

——, 'Caxton's Printing of Chaucer's *Boece*', in *Chaucer in Perspective: Middle English Essays in Honour of Norman Blake*, ed. by Geoffrey Lester (Sheffield: Sheffield Academic Press, 1999), pp. 73–99

Doyle, A. I., 'The Work of a Late Fifteenth-Century English Scribe, William Ebesham', *Bulletin of the John Rylands Library*, 39 (1956–57), 298–325

——, and M. B. Parkes, 'The Production of Copies of the *Canterbury Tales* and the *Confessio Amantis* in the Early Fifteenth Century', in *Medieval Scribes, Manuscripts and Libraries: Essays Presented to N. R. Ker*, ed. by M. B. Parkes and Andrew G. Watson (London: Scolar Press, 1978), pp. 163–210

Edmunds, Sheila, 'From Schoeffer to Vérard: Concerning the Scribes Who Became Printers', in *Printing the Written Word: The Social History of Books, circa 1450–1520*, ed. by Sandra Hindman (Ithaca, NY: Cornell University Press, 1991), pp. 21–40

Edwards, A. S. G., 'Middle English Romance: The Limits of Editing, the Limits of Criticism', in *Medieval Literature: Texts and Interpretation*, ed. by Tim William Machan, Medieval & Renaissance Texts & Studies, 79 (Binghamton, NY: Center for Medieval and Early Renaissance Studies, 1991), pp. 91–104

——, and Carol M. Meale, 'The Marketing of Printed Books in Late Medieval England', *Library*, 6th ser. 15 (1993), 95–124

——, 'Middle English Literature', in *Scholarly Editing: A Guide to Research*, ed. by D. G. Greetham (New York: Modern Language Association of America, 1995), pp. 184–203

——, and Elizabeth Archibald, eds, *A Companion to Malory*, Arthurian Studies, 37 (Cambridge: Brewer, 1996)

Eisenstein, Elizabeth L., *The Printing Press as an Agent of Change: Communications and Cultural Transformations in Early-Modern Europe*, 2 vols (Cambridge: Cambridge University Press, 1979)

——, *The Printing Revolution in Early Modern Europe* (Cambridge: Cambridge University Press, 1983)

Evans, Murray J., 'The Explicits and Narrative Division in the Winchester MS: A Critique of Vinaver's Malory', *Philological Quarterly*, 58 (1979), 263–81

——, 'The Two Scribes in the Winchester MS: The Ninth Explicit and Malory's "Hoole Book"', *Manuscripta*, 27 (1983), 38–44

——, 'Ordinatio and Narrative Links: The Impact of Malory's Tales as a "hoole book"', in *Studies in Malory*, ed. by James W. Spisak (Kalamazoo: Medieval Institute Publications, Western Michigan University, 1985), pp. 29–52

Field, P. J. C., 'Review of *The Works of Sir Thomas Malory*, ed. by Eugène Vinaver', *Studia Neophilologica*, 41 (1969), 180–84

——, 'Thomas Malory: The Hutton Documents', *Medium Aevum*, 48 (1979), 213–39

——, 'The Last Years of Sir Thomas Malory', *Bulletin of the John Rylands Library*, 64 (1982), 433–56

——, 'Review of *Caxton's Malory: A New Edition of Sir Thomas Malory's 'Le Morte Darthur' Based on the Pierpont Morgan Copy of William Caxton's Edition of 1485*, ed. by James W. Spisak', *Library*, 6th ser. 7 (1985), 366–69

——, 'Note to the Third Edition', in *The Works of Sir Thomas Malory*, ed. by Eugène Vinaver, 3rd edn, rev. by P. J. C. Field, 3 vols (Oxford: Clarendon Press, 1990), pp. 1747–68

——, 'Preface to the Third Edition', in *The Works of Sir Thomas Malory*, ed. by Eugène Vinaver, 3rd edn, rev. by P. J. C. Field, 3 vols (Oxford: Clarendon Press, 1990), p. v

——, 'Author, Scribe, and Reader in Malory: The Case of Harleuse and Peryne', in *Noble and Joyous Histories: English Romances 1375–1650*, ed. by Eiléan ní Cuilleanáin and J. D. Pheifer (Dublin: Irish Academic Press, 1993), pp. 137–55

——, 'The Earliest Texts of Malory's *Morte Darthur*', *Poetica*, 38 (1993), 18–31

——, *The Life and Times of Sir Thomas Malory*, Arthurian Studies, 29 (Cambridge: Brewer, 1993)

——, 'Caxton's Roman War', *Arthuriana*, 5.2 (1995), 31–73

——, 'The Malory Life-Records', in *A Companion to Malory*, ed. by Elizabeth Archibald and A. S. G. Edwards, Arthurian Studies, 37 (Cambridge: Brewer, 1996), pp. 115–30

——, 'Review of *The Two Versions of Malory's 'Morte Darthur': Multiple Negation and the Editing of the Text*, by Ingrid Tieken-Boon van Ostade', *Review of English Studies*, n.s. 48 (1997), 518–19

——, ed., *Malory: Texts and Sources*, Arthurian Studies, 40 (Cambridge: Brewer, 1998)

——, 'Balin and the Dolorous Stroke', *"A Ful Noble Knyght": A Medieval Newsletter Devoted to the Life and Art of Sir Thomas Malory*, 1.2 (1999), 1–3

Fish, Jennifer L., and D. Thomas Hanks, Jr., 'Beside the Point: Medieval Meanings vs. Modern Imposition in Editing Malory's *Morte Darthur*', *Neuphilologische Mitteilungen*, 3rd ser. 98 (1997), 273–89

Gaines, Barry, ed., *Sir Thomas Malory: An Anecdotal Bibliography of Editions, 1485–1985* (New York: AMS Press, 1990)

Garbáty, Thomas J., 'Wynkyn de Worde's "Sir Thopas" and Other Tales', *Studies in Bibliography*, 31 (1978), 57–67

Gaskell, Philip, *A New Introduction to Bibliography: The Classic Manual of Bibliography* (1972; repr. Winchester: St Paul's Bibliographies; New Castle, DE: Oak Knoll Press, 1995)

Goodman, Jennifer R., *Malory and William Caxton's Prose Romances of 1485* (New York: Garland, 1987)

Greg, W. W., 'The Early Printed Editions of the *Canterbury Tales*', *PMLA*, 39 (1924), 737–61

——, 'The Rationale of Copy-Text', in *Collected Papers by W. W. Greg*, ed. by J. C. Maxwell (Oxford: Clarendon Press, 1966), pp. 374–91 (first publ. in *Studies in Bibliography*, 3 (1950–51), 19–36)

Griffith, Richard R., 'The Authorship Question Reconsidered: A Case for Thomas Malory of Papworth St Agnes, Cambridgeshire', in *Aspects of Malory*, ed. by Toshiyuki Takamiya and Derek Brewer, Arthurian Studies, 1 (Cambridge: Brewer, 1981), pp. 159–77 and 225–29

——, 'Caxton's Copy-Text for *Le Morte Darthur*: Tracing the Provenance', in *Traditions and Innovations: Essays on British Literature of the Middle Ages and the Renaissance*, ed. by David G. Allen and Robert A. White (Newark: University of Delaware Press, 1990), pp. 75–87

Hanks, D. Thomas, Jr., and Jennifer L. Fish, 'Beside the Point: Medieval Meanings vs. Modern Imposition in Editing Malory's *Morte Darthur*', *Neuphilologische Mitteilungen*, 3rd ser. 98 (1997), 273–89

Hector, L. C., *The Handwriting of English Documents*, 2nd edn (London: Arnold, 1966)

Hellinga, Lotte, 'The Malory Manuscript and Caxton', in *Aspects of Malory*, ed. by Toshiyuki Takamiya and Derek Brewer, Arthurian Studies, 1 (Cambridge: Brewer, 1981), pp. 127–41 and 220–21 (first publ. in *British Library Journal*, 3 (1977), 91–101)

——, *Caxton in Focus: The Beginning of Printing in England* (London: British Library, 1982)

——, 'Manuscripts in the Hands of Printers', in *Manuscripts in the Fifty Years after the Invention of Printing*, ed. by J. B. Trapp (London: Warburg Institute, 1983), pp. 3–11

——, 'Review of *The Two Versions of Malory's 'Morte Darthur': Multiple Negation and the Editing of the Text*, by Ingrid Tieken-Boon van Ostade', *Library*, 6th ser. 19 (1997), 85–87

Hicks, Edward, *Sir Thomas Malory: His Turbulent Career* (1928; New York: Octagon Books, 1970)

Hinman, Charlton, Introduction to *The First Folio of Shakespeare*, The Norton Facsimile (New York: Norton, 1968), pp. ix–xxvii

Hirsch, Rudolf, 'Scribal Tradition and Innovation in Early Printed Books', in *The Printed Word: Its Impact and Diffusion: Primarily in the 15th–16th Centuries*, ed. by Rudolf Hirsch (London: Variorum Reprints, 1978), chapter 15, pp. 1–40

Hutmacher, William F., *Wynkyn de Worde and Chaucer's 'Canterbury Tales': A Transcription and Collation of the 1498 Edition with Caxton² from the General Prologue through the Knight's Tale* (Amsterdam: Rodopi, 1978)

Isaka, Hitoshi, and Yoshihiro Shiratori, 'A Study of "and" in Caxton's *Morte Darthur*', *Round Table*, 11 (1996), 14–30 [in Japanese]

Kane, George, Introduction to *Piers Plowman: The A Version: Will's Visions of Piers Plowman and do-Well* (1960; rev. London: Athlone Press; Berkeley, CA: University of California Press, 1988), pp. 1–172

——, 'Conjectural Emendation', in *Medieval Literature and Civilization: Studies in Memory of G. N. Garmonsway*, ed. by D. A. Pearsall and R. A. Waldron (London: Athlone Press, 1969), pp. 155–69

Kato, Tomomi, ed., *A Concordance to 'The Works of Sir Thomas Malory'* (Tokyo: University of Tokyo Press, 1974)

——, 'Some Scribal Differences in Malory', in *Arthurian and Other Studies Presented to Shunichi Noguchi*, ed. by Takashi Suzuki and Tsuyoshi Mukai (Cambridge: Brewer, 1993), pp. 189–99

Kashiwabara, Kaori, and Kumiko Nishida, 'A Study of Caxton's Punctuation Observed in Malory's *Morte Darthur*', *Round Table*, 11 (1996), 44–50 [in Japanese]

Keiser, George R., 'The Romances', in *Middle English Prose: A Critical Guide to Major Authors and Genres*, ed. by A. S. G. Edwards (New Brunswick, NJ: Rutgers University Press, 1984), pp. 271–89

Kelliher, Hilton, 'The Early History of the Malory Manuscript', in *Aspects of Malory*, ed. by Toshiyuki Takamiya and Derek Brewer, Arthurian Studies, 1 (Cambridge: Brewer, 1981), pp. 143–58 and 222–25

Ker, N. R., Introduction to *The Winchester Malory: A Facsimile*, EETS SS 4 (London: Oxford University Press, 1976), pp. ix–xxii

Kerling, Nelly J. M., 'Caxton and the Trade in Printed Books', *Book Collector*, 4 (1955), 190–99

Kindrick, Robert L., Bonnie Wheeler and Michael N. Salda, eds, *The Malory Debate: Essays on the Texts of 'Le Morte Darthur'*, Arthurian Studies, 47 (Cambridge: Brewer, 2000)

Kurihara, Rie, 'Wood Blocks for Capitals in Caxton's *Morte Darthur*', *Round Table*, 10 (1995), 30–42 [in Japanese]

Laing, Margaret, and Michael Benskin, 'Translations and *Mischsprachen* in Middle English Manuscripts', in *So meny people longages and tonges: Philological Essays in Scots and Mediaeval English Presented to Angus McIntosh*, ed. by Michael Benskin and M. L. Samuels (Edinburgh: Benskin & Samuels, 1981), pp. 55–106

Lewis, C. S., 'The English Prose *Morte*', in *Essays on Malory*, ed. by J. A. W. Bennett (Oxford: Clarendon Press, 1963), pp. 7–28

Life, Page West, ed., *Sir Thomas Malory and the 'Morte Darthur': A Survey of Scholarship and Annotated Bibliography* (Charlottesville: University Press of Virginia, 1980)

Lucas, Peter J., 'Sense-Units and the Use of Punctuation-Markers in John Capgrave's *Chronicle*', *Archivum Linguisticum*, n.s. 2 (1971), 1–24

Lumiansky, R. M., ed., *Malory's Originality: A Critical Study of 'Le Morte Darthur'* (Baltimore: Hopkins, 1964)

McCarthy, Terence, 'Order of Composition in the *Morte Darthur*', *Yearbook of English Studies*, 1 (1971), 18–29

——, 'Caxton and the Text of Malory's Book 2', *Modern Philology*, 71 (1973), 144–52

——, 'The Sequence of Malory's Tales', in *Aspects of Malory*, ed. by Toshiyuki Takamiya and Derek Brewer, Arthurian Studies, 1 (Cambridge: Brewer, 1981), pp. 107–24 and 218–19

McKerrow, Ronald B., *An Introduction to Bibliography for Literary Students*, intro. by David McKitterick (1927; repr. Winchester: St Paul's Bibliographies; New Castle, DE: Oak Knoll Press, 1994)

Martin, Henri-Jean, *The History and Power of Writing*, trans. by Lydia G. Cochrane (Chicago: University of Chicago Press, 1994)

Matheson, Lister M., 'Printer and Scribe: Caxton, the *Polychronicon*, and the *Brut*', *Speculum*, 60 (1985), 593–614

Matthews, William, 'Caxton and Malory: A Defense', in *Medieval Literature and Folklore Studies: Essays in Honor of Francis Lee Utley*, ed. by Jerome Mandel and Bruce A. Rosenberg (New Brunswick, NJ: Rutgers University Press, 1970), pp. 77–96

——, 'Variant Printing in *Le Morte Darthur*', *Library*, 5th ser. 30 (1975), 45–47

——, 'The Besieged Printer', *Arthuriana*, 7.1 (1997), 63–92

——, 'Caxton and Malory: A Re-View', *Arthuriana*, 7.1 (1997), 31–62

——, 'A Question of Texts', *Arthuriana*, 7.1 (1997), 93–133

Meale, Carol M., 'Wynkyn de Worde's Setting-Copy for *Ipomydon*', *Studies in Bibliography*, 35 (1982), 156–71

——, 'Manuscripts, Readers and Patrons in Fifteenth-Century England: Sir Thomas Malory and Arthurian Romance', in *Arthurian Literature IV*, ed. by Richard Barber (Woodbridge: Brewer, 1985), pp. 93–126

——, 'Caxton, de Worde, and the Publication of Romance in Late Medieval England', *Library*, 6th ser. 14 (1992), 283–98

——, and A. S. G. Edwards, 'The Marketing of Printed Books in Late Medieval England', *Library*, 6th ser. 15 (1993), 95–124

——, '"The Hoole Book": Editing and the Creation of Meaning in Malory's Text', in *A Companion to Malory*, ed. by Elizabeth Archibald and A. S. G. Edwards, Arthurian Studies, 37 (Cambridge: Brewer, 1996), pp. 3–17

Mizobata, Kiyokazu, ed., *A Concordance to Caxton's Own Prose* (Tokyo: Shohakusha, 1990)

Moxon, Joseph, *Mechanick Exercises on the Whole Art of Printing*, ed. by Herbert Davis and Harry Carter (1683–84; London: Oxford University Press, 1958)

Mukai, Tsuyoshi, '*Review of Caxton's Malory: A New Edition of Sir Thomas Malory's 'Le Morte Darthur' Based on the Pierpont Morgan Copy of William Caxton's Edition of 1485*, ed. by James W. Spisak', *Studies in English Literature*, English Number (1986), 85–99

——, 'De Worde's Displacement of Malory's Secularization', in *Arthurian and Other Studies Presented to Shunichi Noguchi*, ed. by Takashi Suzuki and Tsuyoshi Mukai (Cambridge: Brewer, 1993), pp. 179–87

——, 'De Worde's 1498 *Morte Darthur* and Caxton's Copy-Text', *Review of English Studies*, n.s. 51 (2000), 24–40

Nagai, Yohko, 'Caxton Reconsidered: Variants between the Morgan Copy and the John Rylands Copy of the *Morte Darthur*', *Round Table*, 10 (1995), 1–16

Nakao, Yuji, 'Does Malory Really Revise his Vocabulary?: Some Negative Evidence', *Poetica*, 25–26 (1987), 93–109

——, 'On the Relationship between the Winchester Malory and Caxton's Malory', in *Arthurian and Other Studies Presented to Shunichi Noguchi*, ed. by Takashi Suzuki and Tsuyoshi Mukai (Cambridge: Brewer, 1993), pp. 201–09

——, 'Musings on the Reviser of Book V in Caxton's Malory', in *The Malory Debate: Essays on the Texts of 'Le Morte Darthur'*, ed. by Bonnie Wheeler, Robert L. Kindrick and Michael N. Salda, Arthurian Studies, 47 (Cambridge: Brewer, 2000), pp. 191–216

Needham, Paul, Introduction to *'Le Morte D'Arthur', Printed by William Caxton 1485: Facsimile* (London: Scolar Press, 1976)

——, *The Printer & the Pardoner* (Washington: Library of Congress, 1986)

Nishida, Kumiko, and Kaori Kashiwabara, 'A Study of Caxton's Punctuation Observed in Malory's *Morte Darthur*', *Round Table*, 11 (1996), 44–50 [in Japanese]

Nixon, Howard M., 'William Caxton and Bookbinding', *Journal of the Printing Historical Society*, 11 (1976–77), 92–113

Noguchi, Shunichi, 'Caxton's Malory', *Poetica*, 8 (1977), 72–84

——, 'Caxton's Malory Again', *Poetica*, 20 (1984), 33–38

——, 'The Winchester Malory as a Scribal (Rather Than an Edited) Text', a paper presented in the Symposium, 'Textual Problems of Malory's *Morte Darthur*', at the Thirteenth Congress of the Japan Society for Medieval English Studies, Seijo University, Tokyo, 7 December 1997

Oakeshott, W. F., 'The Finding of the Manuscript', in *Essays on Malory*, ed. by J. A. W. Bennett (Oxford: Clarendon Press, 1963), pp. 1–6

——, 'The Matter of Malory', *Times Literary Supplement*, 18 February 1977, p. 193

Olefsky, Ellyn, 'Chronology, Factual Consistency, and the Problem of Unity in Malory', *Journal of English and Germanic Philology*, 68 (1969), 57–73

Painter, George D., *William Caxton: A Quincentenary Biography of England's First Printer* (London: Chatto & Windus, 1976)

Parkes, M. B., and A. I. Doyle, 'The Production of Copies of the *Canterbury Tales* and the *Confessio Amantis* in the Early Fifteenth Century', in *Medieval Scribes, Manuscripts and Libraries: Essays Presented to N. R. Ker*, ed. by M. B. Parkes and Andrew G. Watson (London: Scolar Press, 1978), pp. 163–210

——, 'The Influence of the Concepts of *Ordinatio* and *Compilatio* on the Development of the Book', in *Scribes, Scripts and Readers: Studies in the Communication, Presentation and Dissemination of Medieval Texts*, ed. by M. B. Parkes (London: Hambledon, 1991), pp. 35–70

——, *Pause and Effect: An Introduction to the History of Punctuation in the West* (Aldershot: Scolar Press, 1992)

Patterson, Lee, 'The Logic of Textual Criticism and the Way of Genius: The Kane-Donaldson *Piers Plowman* in Historical Perspective', in *Textual Criticism and Literary Interpretation*, ed. by Jerome J. McGann (Chicago: University of Chicago Press, 1985), pp. 55–91

Pearsall, Derek, 'The English Romance in the Fifteenth Century', *Essays and Studies*, n.s. 29 (1976), 56–83

——, 'Editing Medieval Texts: Some Developments and Some Problems', in *Textual Criticism and Literary Interpretation*, ed. by Jerome J. McGann (Chicago: University of Chicago Press, 1985), pp. 92–106

Petti, Anthony G., *English Literary Hands from Chaucer to Dryden* (London: Arnold, 1977)

Pickford, Cedric E., 'An Arthurian Manuscript in the John Rylands Library', *Bulletin of the John Rylands Library*, 31 (1948), 318–44

Pollard, Graham, 'The Names of Some English Fifteenth-Century Binders', *Library*, 5th ser. 25 (1970), 193–218

——, 'The *Pecia* System in the Medieval Universities', in *Medieval Scribes, Manuscripts and Libraries: Essays Presented to N. R. Ker*, ed. by M. B. Parks and Andrew G. Watson (London: Scolar Press, 1978), pp. 145–61

——, 'The English Market for Printed Books', *Publishing History*, 4 (1978), 7–48

Prosser, Eleanor, *Shakespeare's Anonymous Editors: Scribe and Compositor in the Folio Text of '2 Henry IV'* (Stanford, CA: Stanford University Press, 1981)

Reeve, M. D., 'Manuscripts Copied from Printed Books', in *Manuscripts in the Fifty Years after the Invention of Printing*, ed. by J. B. Trapp (London: Warburg Institute, 1983), pp. 12–20

Riddy, Felicity, *Sir Thomas Malory* (Leiden: Brill, 1987)

Rouse, M. A., and R. H. Rouse, '*Ordinatio* and *Compilatio* Revisited', in *Ad Litteram: Authoritative Texts and their Medieval Readers*, ed. by Mark D. Jordan and Kent Emery, Jr. (Notre Dame: University of Notre Dame Press, 1992), pp. 113–34

Rouse, R. H., and M. A. Rouse, '*Ordinatio* and *Compilatio* Revisited', in *Ad Litteram: Authoritative Texts and their Medieval Readers*, ed. by Mark D. Jordan and Kent Emery, Jr. (Notre Dame: University of Notre Dame Press, 1992), pp. 113–34

Ruysschaert, José, 'Les Manuscrits autographes de deux oeuvres de Lorenzo Guglielmo Traversagni imprimées chez Caxton', *Bulletin of the John Rylands Library*, 36 (1953–54), 191–97

Salda, Michael N., Bonnie Wheeler and Robert L. Kindrick, eds, *The Malory Debate: Essays on the Texts of 'Le Morte Darthur'*, Arthurian Studies, 47 (Cambridge: Brewer, 2000)

Sandved, A. O., *Studies in the Language of Caxton's Malory and that of the Winchester Manuscript* (Oslo: Norwegian Universities Press, 1968)

Shaw, Sally, 'Caxton and Malory', in *Essays on Malory*, ed. by J. A. W. Bennett (Oxford: Clarendon Press, 1963), pp. 114–45

Shiratori, Yoshihiro, and Hitoshi Isaka, 'A Study of "and" in Caxton's *Morte Darthur*', *Round Table*, 11 (1996), 14–30 [in Japanese]

Simko, Ján, *Word-Order in the Winchester Manuscript and in William Caxton's Edition of Thomas Malory's 'Morte Darthur' (1485): A Comparison* (Halle: Niemeyer, 1957)

Smith, Jeremy J., 'Some Spellings in Caxton's Malory', *Poetica*, 24 (1986), 58–63

Spisak, James W., ed., *Studies in Malory* (Kalamazoo: Medieval Institute Publications, Western Michigan University, 1985)

——, Introduction to *Caxton's Malory: A New Edition of Sir Thomas Malory's 'Le Morte Darthur' Based on the Pierpont Morgan Copy of William Caxton's Edition of 1485*, ed. by James W. Spisak and William Matthews, with a Dictionary of Names and Places by Bert Dillon, 2 vols (Berkeley, CA: University of California Press, 1983), pp. 601–29

Sutton, Anne F., 'Malory in Newgate: A New Document', *Library*, 7th ser. 1 (2000), 243–62

Takagi, Masako, 'Rubricated Letters in the Winchester Manuscript and Caxton's Textual Divisions', *Round Table*, 12 (1997), 1–65 [in Japanese]

——, and Toshiyuki Takamiya, 'Caxton Edits the Roman War Episode: The *Chronicles of England* and Caxton's Book V', in *The Malory Debate: Essays on the Texts of 'Le Morte Darthur'*, ed. by Bonnie Wheeler, Robert L. Kindrick and Michael N. Salda, Arthurian Studies, 47 (Cambridge: Brewer, 2000), pp. 169–90

Takamiya, Toshiyuki, and Derek Brewer, eds, *Aspects of Malory*, Arthurian Studies, 1 (Cambridge: Brewer, 1981)

——, 'Caxton's Malory Re-edited', *Poetica*, 21–22 (1985), 48–70

——, 'Editor / Compositor at Work: The Case of Caxton's Malory', in *Arthurian and Other Studies Presented to Shunichi Noguchi*, ed. by Takashi Suzuki and Tsuyoshi Mukai (Cambridge: Brewer, 1993), pp. 143–51

——, 'Chapter Divisions and Page Breaks in Caxton's *Morte Darthur*', *Poetica*, 45 (1996), 63–78

——, 'Why a New Edition of the *Morte Darthur*?', a paper presented at the Annual General Meeting of the English Literary Society of Japan, Taisho University, Tokyo, 25 May 1996 [in Japanese]

——, 'Caxton's Copy-fitting Devices in the *Morte Darthur* (1485): An Overview', in *Chaucer in Perspective: Middle English Essays in Honour of Norman Blake*, ed. by Geoffrey Lester (Sheffield: Sheffield Academic Press, 1999), pp. 358–74

——, and Masako Takagi, 'Caxton Edits the Roman War Episode: The *Chronicles of England* and Caxton's Book V', in *The Malory Debate: Essays on the Texts of 'Le Morte Darthur'*, ed. by Bonnie Wheeler, Robert L. Kindrick and Michael N. Salda, Arthurian Studies, 47 (Cambridge: Brewer, 2000), pp. 169–90

Tanselle, G. Thomas, 'Literary Editing', in *Literary and Historical Editing*, ed. by George L. Vogt and John Bush Jones (Lawrence: University of Kansas Libraries, 1981), pp. 35–56

——, 'Classical, Biblical and Medieval Textual Criticism and Modern Editing', *Studies in Bibliography*, 36 (1983), 21–68

Tieken-Boon van Ostade, Ingrid, *The Two Versions of Malory's 'Morte Darthur': Multiple Negation and the Editing of the Text*, Arthurian Studies, 35 (Cambridge: Brewer, 1995)

Tokunaga, Satoko, 'The Sources of Wynkyn de Word's Version of "The Monk's Tale" ',
    Library, 7th ser. 2 (2001), 223–35
Vinaver, Eugène, 'Malory's *Morte Darthur* in the Light of a Recent Discovery', *Bulletin of the
    John Rylands Library*, 19 (1935), 438–57
——, 'A Note on the Earliest Printed Texts of Malory's *Morte Darthur*', *Bulletin of the John
    Rylands Library*, 23 (1939), 102–06
——, 'Principles of Textual Emendation', in *Medieval Manuscripts and Textual Criticism*, ed.
    by Christopher Kleinhenz, North Carolina Studies in the Romance Languages and
    Literatures Symposia, 4 (1939; Chapel Hill: North Carolina Studies in the Romance
    Languages and Literatures, UNC Department of Romance Languages, 1976), pp. 139–
    66
——, 'Critical Approaches to Medieval Romance', in *Literary History and Literary Criticism*,
    ed. by Leon Edel (New York: New York University Press, 1965), pp. 16–27
——, Introduction to *The Works of Sir Thomas Malory*, ed. by Eugène Vinaver, 3rd edn, rev.
    by P. J. C. Field, 3 vols (1947; Oxford: Clarendon Press, 1990), pp. xix–cxxvi
Wheeler, Bonnie, Robert L. Kindrick and Michael N. Salda, eds, *The Malory Debate: Essays
    on the Texts of 'Le Morte Darthur'*, Arthurian Studies, 47 (Cambridge: Brewer, 2000)
Wilson, Robert H., 'Review of *The Works of Sir Thomas Malory*, ed. by Eugène Vinaver',
    Modern Philology, 46 (1948), 136–38
——, 'Malory and Caxton', in *A Manual of the Writings in Middle English 1050–1500*, ed. by
    Albert E. Hartung and others, vol. 3 (New Haven, CT: The Connecticut Academy of
    Arts and Sciences, 1972), pp. 757–807 and 909–51
Withrington, John, 'Caxton, Malory, and the Roman War in the *Morte Darthur*', *Studies in
    Philology*, 89 (1992), 350–66